PLAYBOOK FOR PROGRESSIVES

PLAYBOOK FOR PROGRESSIVES

16 Qualities of the Successful Organizer

Eric Mann

BEACON PRESS, BOSTON

Beacon Press
25 Beacon Street
Boston, Massachusetts 02108-2892
www.beacon.org

Beacon Press books
are published under the auspices of
the Unitarian Universalist Association of Congregations.

14 13 12 11   8 7 6 5 4 3 2 1

This book is printed on acid-free paper that meets the uncoated paper
ANSI/NISO specifications for permanence as revised in 1992.

Text design by Yvonne Tsang at
Wilsted & Taylor Publishing Services

Library of Congress Cataloging-in-Publication Data

Mann, Eric.
Playbook for progressives : 16 qualities of the successful organizer /
Eric Mann.
p. cm.
ISBN 978-0-8070-4735-4 (pbk. : alk. paper)
1. Community organization. 2. Social action—Planning.
3. Political participation. 4. Social movements. 5. Political activists.
6. Leadership. I. Title.
HM766.M36 2011
322.4—dc22   2010050224

Some names and identifying characteristics of people mentioned
in this work have been changed to protect their identities.

For

Lian Hurst Mann and Daniel Won-gu Kim.
You were there from the first word to the last.
This book is our work.

CONTENTS

INTRODUCTION

"Down South I've been beaten three times since I joined SNCC. I've been thrown in jail for no good reason and beaten again once I was in there. The police and the Klan threatened to kill me and when they said that, I believed them." This young Black man from the Student Nonviolent Coordinating Committee (SNCC), no older than eighteen or nineteen, is challenging his audience from the steps of Willard Straight Hall at Cornell University. It is 1963, and the long winter is giving way. Far above Cayuga Lake, the sun illuminates the bridges across the rocky gorges. The grass is already green. The young man is pointing to every one of us: "I'm tired of the way you think I'm exaggerating; I'm tired of how little you give of your life when you can give so much more. Unless there is a lot of support from the North, a lot of us are gonna get killed because we register voters and organize people for their civil rights. My question to you is this: Who among you will join the civil rights revolution?" I think for only a moment and understand I have come to a conclusion: "I will!"

It was an evangelical call. What a gift it was. In 1964, I graduated from Cornell and got a job as a field secretary for the Congress of Racial Equality (CORE) in the North. I was put to work helping to organize a boycott of the Trailways Bus Company, fighting to integrate its segregated workforce, and, as I'll tell you about more in the pages of this book, we won. Joining the civil rights revolution was my induction into *transformative organizing,* a tradition of building social movements to challenge the entire system that defines U.S. history and the present.

Transformative organizing recruits masses of people to fight militantly for immediate concrete demands that have to be won—integrating segregated facilities, getting jobs for Black people, shutting down military recruiting on a campus—but always as part of a larger strategy to change structural conditions in the world: To end post-slavery apartheid. To stop a war. To build a powerful, long-term movement. *Transformative organizing works to transform the system, transform the consciousness of the people being organized, and, in the process, transform the consciousness of the organizer.* It is the backbone and the model of what we are fighting for and how we can succeed in that battle.

For the two decades of the 1960s—from the 1955 Montgomery bus boycott and the Bandung Conference of non-aligned nations to the final victory of the Vietnamese people in 1975—the practice of transformative organizing grew exponentially. It was a period of world uprising and revolution. In the United States, there was an explosion of self-organization as thousands of collectives, organizations, communes, and campaigns were built, involving millions of people who considered themselves part of "the Movement." Black people expressed their rage against the system through rebellions in 458 cities between 1965 and 1967 alone.

Transformative organizing was essential to one of the signal achievements of this period. A full one hundred years after the legal abolition of slavery, the Black community, the Black Nation, led a united front with the New Left to fight against conditions of semi-slavery, enforced poverty, legal Jim Crow in the South, and de facto segregation in the North, all enforced by a police and Klan terror so inextricably linked that civil rights workers described it as "blue by day, white by night." The Movement won the passage of the 1964 Civil

Rights Act and the 1965 Voting Rights Act, significant state restriction on Klan activity, and reduction of some of the worst police abuses. They won open housing and school integration programs, fair employment laws and affirmative action programs, and the right to vote protected by the federal government. The Movement won through sit-ins, marches, freedom rides, recruiting through hundreds of thousands of one-on-one conversations, training organizers, and the support of a world Left that denounced U.S. racism in the midst of the Cold War. A militant and unified Black people, brought to the United States in chains, were able to lead a broad united front to finally overthrow three hundred years of formal racial segregation and apartheid in its most legalized and overt form. This required a literal revolution against the culture, institutions, and laws of U.S. society.

This connection between ideology on one hand and strategy and tactics on the other is one of the hallmarks of transformative organizing. Ideology is a worldview that gives the most essential direction to your life and leads organizations in their work to change conditions in the world.

Let me give an example. In April 1965, Students for a Democratic Society (SDS) called for a march against the war in Vietnam to be held on the big lawn in front of the Washington Monument. The United States already had 100,000 troops in Vietnam and was moving to escalate its presence to 184,000 troops. President Lyndon Baines Johnson had run as the peace candidate and had promised, in the election of 1964 versus the arch war-hawk Barry Goldwater, to de-escalate the war. In a classic betrayal, Johnson broke his electoral promise and initiated massive aerial bombing of north Vietnam in February 1965, killing hundreds of thousands of Vietnamese men, women, and children, almost all civilians, in a bloody effort to terrorize them to surrender. The war forced itself onto the consciousness of the Civil Rights Movement especially, and SNCC proposed that Black people should not fight in the war even when drafted using the slogan "Hell No, We Won't Go."

While the march organizers had hoped for five thousand attendees, for this was the early stages of the antiwar movement, and feared many fewer would show, on April 4, more than thirty thousand people attended, with bus loads from New York, Michigan, and the far West.

I attended the rally at a time when public oratory was one of the great educative tools. Four speakers created a talking book, with each one writing a chapter that was part of an integrated social theory. I.F. Stone, the iconoclastic journalist, warned us, "Do not trust the government's lies about Vietnam. Develop your own research, your own magazines, your own newspapers, your own sources." Staughton Lynd, a pacifist professor from Yale, challenged us to take courageous actions to stop an immoral war. Using the call from the Civil Rights Movement, he urged us to "put your bodies on the line." Robert Moses from SNCC told us that the civil rights and antiwar struggles were two fronts in a wider war against racism and colonialism—"Make the connections between segregation in the South and defoliation in the Third World."

Paul Potter, the twenty-five-year-old president of SDS, gave a stirring speech that shaped the consciousness of the attendees and lives in my mind to this day.

> The incredible war in Vietnam has provided the razor, the terrifying, sharp, cutting edge that has finally severed the last vestige of illusion that morality and democracy are the guiding principles of American foreign policy. . . . That is a terrible and bitter insight for people who grew up as we did—and our revulsion at that insight, our refusal to accept it as inevitable or necessary, is one of the reasons that so many people have come here today. . . .
>
> We must name that system. We must name it, describe it, analyze it, understand it, and change it. For it is only when that system is changed and brought under control that there can be any hope for stopping

the forces that create a war in Vietnam today or a murder in the South tomorrow or all the incalculable, innumerable, more subtle atrocities that are worked on people all over, all the time.

Thousands of us were called to action in what amounted to a three-hour-long consciousness-raising-group meeting, supported by the musical interventions of Bob Dylan, Joan Baez, Phil Ochs, and the SNCC Freedom Singers. After such a deep ideological transformation, the question was, "What should I do now?"

I decided to sign up for the civil disobedience that was rumored to be taking place after the march to the Capitol steps. With some organizing experience from my work with CORE, some good public-speaking tools, and a strong will to act, I was elected one of the lead organizers and spokespeople for our small band of fifty—the first sit-in in front of the White House against the war in Vietnam.

The words I spoke to my fellow protestors reflected the lessons I had just learned: "This is a personal witness and confrontation with the power structure. We understand the need for a broad-based demonstration, but in order to change a fundamentally rotten system you have to take fundamental action that directly confronts the source of the problem—the Johnson administration and the system itself." We received extensive coverage from the Movement magazine, the *Guardian*. When we were finally removed from our vigil by D.C. police several days later, the Washington and New York papers ran pictures of us being arrested with locked arms as the police lifted us from our nonviolent human chain. The SDS March on Washington was a large-scale tactic in transformative organizing, changing the ideological consciousness of thirty thousand people who in turn went back to their communities to carry out the multiplier effect and organize a stronger antiwar movement. I went back to Newark, New Jersey, where I was an organizer with the Newark Community Union Project (NCUP, pronounced *en-cup*). Our demands of "No Rent for Rats," "Let the People Decide," and "No Police Brutality" expanded to "U.S. Out of Vietnam Now."

In the 1980s, the Right reached its clear ideological apogee with the election of Ronald Reagan, the fall of the Berlin Wall, and the defeat of the Soviet Union. U.S. capitalism went on the military and ideological offensive. Reagan attacked Black women on welfare as "welfare queens." Allan Bakke, a white medical school applicant, spoke for every white who did not want Blacks to get "affirmative action." His spurious claim of "reverse discrimination" was upheld by the Supreme Court. There was a backlash against women's reproductive rights and gay liberation with the glorification of the nuclear family and "family values." A powerful conservative movement came to power in a direct attack on all of the victories of the New Left.

This move to the Right, an actual counterrevolution, began to impact the confidence and orientation of the millions of people who had been on the front lines of the battle for decades. The repression and exhaustion took a toll, and during the 1980s, the defeat of revolutionary movements around the world, combined with the cooptation and repression of many social movements in the United States, led to a period of right-wing triumphalism that has created great demoralization among some progressive activists to this day.

Labor and community organizers began talking about "empowerment" rather than power, "a seat at the table" rather than concrete demands and political independence, and "public-private partnerships" rather than a challenge to the profit motive and corporate power. Instead of building movements critical and independent of the Democratic Party, many grassroots groups became appendages of local elected officials. When asked why the change, they would reply: "The times have changed. We have to be practical. We don't want to be isolated."

The Right seemed to be able to win the debate before it

could even begin. And, yet, few organizers could argue that restricting the scope of their work had increased their effectiveness. Some of the organizers who had initially rejected transformative organizing returned to it. And many young people, who saw themselves on a continuum with the great Left victories of the 1930s and '60s, put forth a far more radical politics, doing great work in low-income communities, and looking for a theory and practice of resistance to the existing system.

Among the groups swimming hard against the conservative tide of the times was a group of us who formed the Labor/ Community Strategy Center in 1989 as a multiracial "think tank/act tank," an experiment to reassert the powerful, positive impact of progressive ideology and transformative organizing. In 1992, in Los Angeles, the car capital of the world, we initiated the Bus Riders Union/Sindicato de Pasajeros (BRU/ SDP) and relit a beacon for transformative organizing.

The Bus Riders Union is a mass membership organization rooted among the 500,000 bus riders in Los Angeles County. The concept of the Bus Riders Union (BRU) came from scores of conversations we pursued with transit officials and bus riders. It did not take long for us to assess that the Los Angeles Metropolitan Transportation Authority (MTA) was setting up a racially discriminatory, two-tiered mass transit system—a highly expensive rail system to benefit contractors, campaign contributors, and, significantly, white suburban commuters, and a dirty, dilapidated, diesel bus system inflicted upon low-income bus riders of color, who represented 92 percent of all the MTA's passengers.

Bus riders' grievances seemed infinite. The buses were late, filthy, decrepit, overcrowded, and running on polluting diesel fuel. The wheelchair lifts constantly broke down, leaving disabled people stranded, and sometimes an entire bus broke down, leaving everyone waiting to be herded into the next already overcrowded bus. At the same time, the MTA was raising the bus fares and eliminating the monthly bus pass to pay for cost overruns on its expensive rail system.

From the outset, we faced several questions as to whether or not our transformative model could be reconstructed in the conservative '90s. We saw the bus as what I called "a factory on wheels," uniting a group of disparate people—hotel and restaurant workers, high school and college students, the disabled, and people from every race, nationality, language, and neighborhood in the city. But would they see themselves as a group, as a multiracial working class?

The L.A. rebellion was just around the corner. Proposition 187 was raising anti-immigrant assaults. If our goal was a Black and Latino alliance, and the largest Asian group was Korean, how could we get communities and cultures often at each other's throats to see each other as allies, then as members of the same organization? Could we initiate the BRU as a movement organization that differed from the more pragmatic, issue-based organizations of the day? Could our small grassroots group sustain what would be a very long campaign against a $3-billion-a-year agency, without breaking up over exhaustion, recrimination, or despair? As organizers always say to each other, "Only practice will tell."

After talks with hundreds of riders, we came up with a clear program of demands: 50-cent fares; $20 monthly bus passes; thousands of new, clean-fuel buses; a seat for every passenger; and an elected MTA board. We also wanted dramatically reduced emissions, low-floor buses for wheelchair access, and bike racks on the buses. Our programmatic demands were framed by transformative slogans we felt could help energize people for what would be a multiyear, protracted battle: "Fight Transit Racism," "Billions for Buses," "Make History."

We began by building a strong core. We found that our strong antiracist politics attracted the most militant Black and Latino riders, and our focus on a union of passengers, "Sindicato de Pasajeros," had particular resonance among immigrants from Latin America with previous trade union backgrounds. Dozens of new members made monthly pilgrimages to the L.A. MTA meetings, where haughty elected officials did their best impression of declining royalty and rejected our demands for more buses and better service. For the next year, we sent dozens of organizers onto MTA buses to talk to thousands of MTA passengers. We marched, picketed, lobbied, educated the public, and had highly publicized sit-ins in protest of MTA policies. Yet the MTA board would not budge.

Finally, in 1994, we took the MTA to court for violating Title VI of the 1964 Civil Rights Act by setting up a separate and unequal transit system that used federal funds in a racially discriminatory manner. We were brilliantly represented by NAACP Legal Defense and Education Fund attorneys Connie Rice, Bill Lann Lee, and Richard Larson. We organized hundreds of bus riders to write depositions documenting racial discrimination and "irreparable harm," a legal standard for immediate judicial intervention. The federal district judge, Terry Hatter, to our shock, issued a temporary restraining order against the MTA, reversed the fare increases, and reinstated the monthly bus pass. We were the lead story on every local media outlet, and this during the height of the O.J. Simpson trial.

We then initiated a transformative tactic. Our yellow-shirted organizers would board buses and tell riders our slogan, "No Seat, No Fare," and urge them, "Don't pay for racism." And if they could not get a seat, "Don't stand for it." Tens of thousands of riders participated, and many bus drivers were very supportive, telling some passengers, "This is a Bus Riders Union No-Seat, No-Fare Campaign bus. You don't have to pay." The MTA called transit police, but the bus drivers would tell the police everything was under control—and so they left. The MTA tried to get a court order to stop the campaign, but the courts refused to intervene. We had won control of the buses of Los Angeles.

Under this kind of pressure, the MTA finally signed a ten-year consent decree with the Bus Riders Union. In it, the MTA agreed to dramatically improve bus service, and the BRU was appointed "class representative" for the interests of, by now, 500,000 bus riders. Even after the signing of the decree, the

MTA was recalcitrant. But we never let up. Through years of op-eds, lawn signs, mass campaigns, testimony, more sit-ins, negotiation with MTA officials, and, most decisively, powerful federal court orders, the MTA grudgingly, always years later, began to buy a significant number of brand-new compressed natural gas (CNG) buses.

Today, when you walk the streets of L.A. and wait at a bus stop, a new CNG-fueled bus, still overcrowded, shows up with low floors for the disabled. There are 2,500 new buses on the roads, and the entire diesel fleet has been retired. Now the MTA boasts it's "the largest clean-fuel bus fleet in the U.S.," *at a cost of $2.5 billion dollars,* which everyone in the city knows they carried out only through the organizing of the Bus Riders Union and federal court orders. We fought transit racism, won billions for buses, and made history.

As for the questions we faced when we started, we have another slogan that guides our organizing at the Strategy Center: "Consciousness, Leadership, and Organization." Over time, the BRU has moved from being a militant civil rights group to a progressive organization rooted on the buses. Check out a monthly membership meeting of the Bus Riders Union. One hundred low-income people will be having the most heated political discussions in Spanish, Korean, and English, or laughing at a joke, all simultaneously translated by professionals through the most modern UN-style headsets. The group is of course attentive to the specifics of our mission—lower bus fares, problems with MTA service, racist practices on the bus. But at the same meeting, there will be a presentation of LGBTQ rights, not an abstract question since a growing number of the young members identify as queer.

The next month, we have a special session where members can get their frustrations off their chests and talk about the daily humiliations of their ride on the bus system and how we can improve that. At the same meeting, people give performances on their instruments, celebrate a birthday, or hold a memorial service for a fallen member. At another meeting, members give a vivid PowerPoint report of their recent trip to Gaza and advocate for Palestinian rights, and at still another, we hold an educational discussion of the wars in Iraq and Afghanistan. After the meeting is over, the members pack lunches and march off to be part of the gay pride parade or the demonstration against the war in Iraq. Our many high school and college students, often the most militant and innovative, lead a chant.

> We're the Bus Riders Union
> And this is our fight,
> Mass transportation is a human right.
> We want fifty-cent fares and twenty-dollar passes,
> 'Cause mass transportation belongs to the masses.

And by now, hundreds of marchers have sought out our Drum and Chant crew, as all the drummers in a ten-thousand-person antiwar march find each other and march together. We have two hundred active members, three thousand dues-paying members, and more than fifty thousand supporters on the bus lines and throughout the county—we are building a movement and a multiracial, multigenerational community. For us, "theory-driven practice" is a popularly embraced concept. It gives focus to our work and allows our members to be in charge of their own destiny.

Out of this work and the work of others across the country, we have formed a new national campaign, Transit Riders for Public Transportation (TRPT), with the Strategy Center, BRU, Urban Habitat and Public Advocates in the San Francisco/ Oakland Bay area, Little Village Environmental Justice Organization in Chicago, West Harlem Environmental Action and UPROSE (United Puerto Rican Organization of Sunset Park) in Brooklyn, and the T Riders Union in Boston. TRPT is a national, environmental justice, mass transportation organization in the United States, focusing on, not surprisingly, transit racism and the development of clean-fuel bus systems that serve all urban residents. We are challenging King Auto's production of greenhouse gases and toxic emissions, and seeking a massive change in federal transit policy from the auto to public transportation.

Strategy Center organizers have visited Ecuador, Venezuela, and South Africa and have been active participants in the UN World Conference against Racism and the World Summit on Sustainable Development. In 2010, we attended the World Conference of the UN Framework on Climate Change in Cochabamba, Bolivia and the sixteenth convening of the UN Framework Convention on Climate Change (UNFCC) in Cancun, Mexico. We know that whatever long-term solutions we are fighting for can only be won with a strong base in Los Angeles and a solid set of national and international allies. As we meet organizers from other U.S. cities, elsewhere in North America, Europe, Africa, and Asia, there is a sense that we need an international movement, especially among grassroots organizers who have such deep ties to low-income and oppressed communities and have had it with efforts to modify or mollify the system.

Transformative organizers are needed more than ever to build vibrant mass movements. Through this book, I will tell you stories about people and events, transformational speakers, activists, and organizers; the long-distance runners whose words and deeds, ideas and actions have changed, and are currently changing, the lives of millions. I will ask you, as the young man asked us more than forty years ago, *Who among you wants to join the social justice revolution?*

Today, hundreds of thousands of organizers and millions of activists are fighting for affordable housing, ending the mass incarceration of Black and Brown youth, reversing toxic and greenhouse gas emissions, expanding LGBTQ rights, protesting the U.S. invasions of Iraq and Afghanistan, and dozens of other heartfelt issues requiring the most radical structural changes. I have talked to hundreds of "issue-based" organizers who feel that their "one cause at a time" approach, which was motivated by a desire to restrict the scope of their demands in order to "win something," has led to isolation, ineffectiveness, and a sense of alienation.

It is possible that the deterioration of U.S. imperialism into its most militaristic and decadent form may provide the impetus for an urgently needed historical development —the strategy of building an international united front against the abuses of the United States. Our survival and that of the planet depends on moving beyond U.S. dominance. Transformative organizers who self-define as liberal, radical, progressive, and revolutionary, including many of us who worked to elect Barack Obama, must come forward to name and change the system—the capitalist system in crisis. We need a new Movement to carry forth a comprehensive political program, as well as a strategy and tactics that can simultaneously build the broadest possible united front and put organizations in the same city, state, and country in truly organized forms, such as strong, disciplined coalitions, networks, alliances, and large campaigns.

Playbook for Progressives is written for a broad audience of people who want to get involved, those who want to accelerate their level of involvement, and those who are already on the front lines of the battle and want to push themselves to a higher level of effectiveness. This book is an experiment in transformative organizing. My hope is that you, the reader, will interrogate and engage the twelve roles of the organizer's job description and the sixteen qualities of the successful organizer. From there, my hope is that you will be transformed, from a critic to an activist, from an activist to an organizer, and, finally, from an organizer to a more conscious, introspective, and successful leader.

PART 1

The Job Description

12 Roles of the Successful Organizer

An organizer is a leader of an organization and is never alone. Whenever there is a successful movement, you will find organizers working with dozens, hundreds, even thousands of other organizers—this was the case during the mass strikes of the Congress of Industrial Organizations in the 1930s, in the mass civil rights marches in the United States, and through the decades of anti-apartheid struggle in South Africa. Today, organizers in low-income Black and Latino communities and in the LGBTQ (lesbian, gay, bisexual, transgender, queer), environmental justice, immigrant rights, and labor movements are coming to understand that *the key to victory is the recruitment, training, and mentoring of a new generation of organizers.*

The job of an organizer is to build a base and lead it effectively to advance an overarching long-term strategy. The goal is to force those in power to do something they would not do otherwise, and it cannot be achieved unless organizers are equipped with a clear ideology and a firm, unambiguous strategy. Look at every successful organization, every successful progressive movement you know. You will find that success begins with a theory of transformative organizing, a long-term strategy, and a tactical plan.

The organizer is the smallest human unit around whom you can build a project, a campaign, an organization. An organizer does not operate as a loner—by her nature she belongs to and is loyal to an organization. The organizer represents the views of the organization with the goal of recruiting new members. Once the members join, the organizer's job is to mentor, sustain, support, and learn from the membership. The transformative organizer brings new people into a movement to challenge the ideology, institutions, and policies of the system and is fighting for the most radical and revolutionary changes.

Before describing the sixteen qualities of the successful organizer, I will first discuss the twelve roles that make up the organizer's job description. Not all organizers need to or can master all roles in this job description. But for those of you who strive to be the senior organizers—the lead organizers—you will need to develop competency and mastery of each role and understand them as different aspects of a unified whole. Organizing at its best is as difficult as brain surgery—it's much easier to get it wrong than to get it right. That's why I highlight the long-distance runners, the activists and organizers, who have invested most of their lives trying to win specific demands and change the system. This requires a lifelong process of practice, study, training, reflection, and more practice.

In the United States in particular, and among organizers in general, there is a pragmatic, antitheoretical tendency: "I don't want to be bogged down in theory. Let me get out on the block and do my job, and I'll learn as I go along." The problem is that theory is an overview that gives you a map as to where you are going. The job of organizer is so difficult, so complex; it involves understanding yourself as a person, understanding the goals and objectives of your organization, understanding and studying the world situation, and trying to figure out, in a world so hard to change, how social change is possible. Isn't it interesting that if you ask an organizer what is involved in the job, she will often tell you, "I don't know. I'm too busy doing it to think about it." But there's the rub. Because being mindful, conscious, of what we do when we wake up every morning is critical to our success. When many of the best organizers in the country read this book, and see the theoretical statement of the job description of the organizer, and later the sixteen qualities of the successful organizer, they will say, "On many levels I knew that; in many ways this is not new information; and yet in many ways it is completely new information, because without consciousness we do not even understand what we do very well and could do so much better." It is in that spirit that the job description of the organizer is disassembled and then reassembled for the benefit of a movement for radical social change, a Movement for Global Justice.

The Foot Soldier

An organizer is situated somewhere in the physical world. Her terrain can be a block in an urban center or a neighborhood, on Soto Street in East Los Angeles or the Lower Ninth Ward in New Orleans, in the recovery room at Brigham and Women's Hospital in Boston or in the foundry at the Ford River Rouge plant outside Detroit. You can find the organizer working the first, second, or third shift at the giant Walmart complex in Albany, New York; advocating with AIDS Project Los Angeles; cleaning the floors and classrooms at Erasmus Hall High School in Brooklyn; organizing antiwar resistance among her fellow soldiers in Baghdad, Iraq. He can be found across the globe in the Mercedes assembly plant in East London or South Africa, with the Petróleos de Venezuela in the Orinoco Belt, or in the main stadium of the Hua Mark Sports Complex in Bangkok, Thailand. The most developed organizers—those in regional and national leadership—have the responsibility to supervise labor, environmental, antiracist, and antiwar organizers in an entire city, region, or country.

The foot soldier works on the ground in her terrain. She goes door-to-door in the community, hangs around the neighborhood *bodega,* and is known by high school students, those working from dawn to dusk, the unemployed who spend the day looking for work, and the women working a fulltime job taking care of their kids. She works in a garment sweatshop and talks to workers on her break or at the factory gate. She gets out on the bus and goes passenger-to-passenger, agitating, evangelizing, recruiting. Bus Riders Union (BRU) organizers go out on the bus for four hours every day. Chanting "Get on the bus, get on the bus, get on the bus, and fight with us," their goal is to recruit new members to the movement.

When I worked with the Newark Community Union Project (NCUP) from 1965 to 1967, my job was to go door-to-door in the housing projects and tenements of the Black South Ward. In the brutal heat of summer and the freezing cold of winter, Jesse Allen, Phil Hutchings, Bessie and Thurman Smith, Corinna Fales, Tom Hayden, Connie Brown, and many more of us had to "get out on the block," knock on doors, sit down with people, explain the program and the organization's mission, and encourage community residents to come to meetings and protests. It didn't take long to dawn on me: "This job is hard."

I met with many Black community residents and listened to their stories. One of my regular contacts was a very brave woman whom I'll call Jessie Terry. Jessie and her three young sons would sit around a stove-like heater in the middle of their living room in the freezing cold. She wanted to offer me some food, but her refrigerator was almost bare. She would bring me hot coffee, and we would sit and talk. Once, perhaps influenced by Martin Luther King Jr.'s metaphor, I asked her if she had a dream of what her life could be like. She told me, "My dream is that I am able to walk in front of a car and leave this life and God will not punish me for abandoning my children."

I was shaken to the bone. I realized that I had no capacity out of my own privileged life to grasp that level of despair. I stretched with all my might to understand her and to offer solace and companionship. I also realized I had no easy solution to her problems besides a general exhortation to "organize." Sadly, I already had learned that her life was not that different from that of the woman next door or across the street. She was a specific reflection of the oppression of Black women and Black people generally in the neighborhood we were working in. Jessie had given me a gift, a vulnerable window into her life, because she knew I would not judge but would struggle to understand. It was her plea to me, as a friend and organizer, and to the movement to change the unbearable conditions of the people in the Newark ghetto. It made me want to work harder, to fight harder, to fight for Jessie and her family. On days when I did not want to go out on the block, I would think of Jessie and push myself to go out and do my job without hesitation or complaint.

Being a successful foot soldier is very hard to do and even harder to sustain. Even when an organizer gets off to a successful and enthusiastic start, it is difficult to evaluate whether he will be successful over the long term—day after day, week after week, year after year. Every experienced organizer has seen would-be organizers realize they can't do the job. The "masses" are not always friendly, and making that connection with people, especially in times of political despair and reaction, is very difficult. Many organizers-in-training have told me, "I was very excited about the idea, but after doing it for a while, I'm starting to realize I don't really have the energy or will to be an organizer." So we discuss other jobs in the organization where they can make a contribution—research, web design, fund-raising, drum and chant crew, political theater, phone banking, office administration, publicity, media. If people are loyal to an organization driven by grassroots organizing, they can still be of great help to the movement. It's the job of an organizer to find the right match between their capacities and the needs of the organization, and to never let a dedicated person get away.

Saladin Muhammad: Black Workers for Justice

Saladin Muhammad understands the role of the foot soldier well. Saladin grew up in Philadelphia, served in the U.S. military from 1962 to 1965, and frequently visited Rocky Mount,

North Carolina, where his aunt lived and where he later met his wife, Naeema. He returned to Rocky Mount in 1981 to initiate a collective of Black organizers who had formerly been with other Black-led formations. He got a job working for a janitorial service that cleaned many factories in the area. As an underground organizer in predominantly Black workplaces, this also gave him access to factories around the city, where he learned about poor working conditions while making new contacts.

At a meeting of support for the Kmart workers, Saladin saw the need for a longer-term campaign and a broader organization of Black workers after listening to the testimony of three Black women. In 1981, Mildred Daisy, Christine Smith, and Helen Solomon sent a petition to improve working conditions, signed by concerned workers, to Kmart's national office in Michigan. They were repaid by being fired. After the meeting, Saladin approached the women to see if they wanted to talk. Out of those conversations, a new organization was born—Black Workers for Justice (BWFJ). They initiated a petition campaign among Black workers in the area, with the ultimate goal of threatening to boycott Kmart if the company did not accede to their demands: that Kmart rehire the women, fire a discriminatory supervisor, and end racially discriminatory practices at the company. In the racist atmosphere of an anti-union state, the petition campaign allowed BWFJ to set up organizing captains in communities and workplaces throughout Rocky Mount.

The petition drive was supported by many Black workers, but Kmart management refused to meet the demands. This led to a boycott campaign that was phenomenally successful, cutting Kmart sales by more than 50 percent. While management would not rehire the workers, this was a big victory in terms of organization building. The Black Workers for Justice further extended its reach, setting up workers' centers at many key workplaces in the region: Standard Products, Hardwood Dimensions (a saw mill whose workers were almost all Black), Phillips Fibers, Consolidated Diesel, and Tex Fie, a textile mill.

Throughout the campaign, Saladin Muhammad was a lead organizer and tireless foot soldier. He woke up at 5:00 a.m. and took petitions to the city workers before they started their shift. After that, he went to meet the sanitation workers at their shape up as they were loading their trucks, before walking the mile to where the city's park and recreation workers were gathering. Saladin organized house meetings of Black working-class families and met with the three fired women and other Kmart workers at least twice a week. Then he would begin his own janitorial job on the swing shift at 5:00 p.m., working until 2:00 a.m. He would go home, get to sleep at about 3:00 a.m., wake up at 5:00 a.m., and start the day all over again, coming back in the afternoon to grab a few winks before he went to work. "Hey, I was young then," he says, "and it was so exciting to see so many Black folks in motion."

Today, thirty years later, Saladin is a theorist, a strategist, a respected national leader of the Black, labor, and progressive movements. And he is still getting out on the block. He now works for the United Electrical Workers Union (UE) with their International Workers Justice Campaign and is still based in Rocky Mount, North Carolina. Their goal is to win collective bargaining rights for city workers in a "right-to-work" anti-union state. He meets with workers, attends city council meetings, and has helped to win a pay raise for the workers on the way to the larger goal of unionization. A long-distance runner, he still goes to the workplace and talks to the workers—the lifeblood of why he continues to fight.

He wanted Black people to come to politics out of self-love and self-respect and a rejection of the culture of colonialism. And he wanted them all to support OAAU and to see that "our problem was no longer a Negro problem or an American problem but a . . . problem for humanity. A problem that was so complex that it was impossible for Uncle Sam to solve it himself." He wanted to bring it before world bodies "before it gets so explosive that no one can handle it." On February 21, 1965, Malcolm X was assassinated. In his few short years of public exposure he had become one of the most compelling figures of the twentieth century, and his speeches in books and on recordings are masterworks of evangelical discourse.

It is no wonder that the actor Ossie Davis, another powerful evangelist, gave one of the greatest speeches in U.S. history, his "Eulogy for Malcolm," on February 27, 1965, at the Faith Temple Church in Harlem. He explained that Malcolm was working in Africa to gain international support for the Afro-American human rights struggle in the United States. He praised Malcolm for "his meticulous use of words" and for his understanding of the power of evangelical strategic thought. He observed that "Malcolm was our manhood, our living Black manhood." He gave Malcolm the highest compliment, as "a prince—our Black shining prince, who didn't hesitate to die because he loved us so."

Many of us trained in this period were shaped by the evangelical approach of Fannie Lou Hamer, Diane Nash, Stokely Carmichael, Kathleen Cleaver, Cleveland Sellers, and tens of thousands of Black civil rights workers. This evangelical pedagogy required the speaker to make a strong connection between the heart, conscience, consciousness, and intellect of his audience. Then and now, the highest compliment you could get from an audience was "Preach, brother, preach. Preach, sister, preach."

The Evangelist

The role of the evangelist is to recruit and retain people in the movement by touching their deepest feelings and aspirations. The evangelist calls for a personal transformation, a conversion of values, a commitment to a larger whole and a broader cause.

Dr. Martin Luther King Jr. is remembered as one of the most influential evangelists. There are some who assume King's evangelical skills were best used in his "I Have a Dream" speech, but King realized his "Dream" speech had placed too much faith in the goodness of white people and in the system itself. He made a tactical decision to present his speeches with a tougher edge, more concrete and resistant to cooptation. In his last years, King experienced a profound conversion—from a militant integrationist to a supporter of Black liberation, from a leader focusing on the plight of Blacks in the United States to an internationalist who saw the plight of Black people in the United States tied to the struggles of the peoples of the Third World. He further shifted from being a private critic of the war in Vietnam to one of its most outspoken opponents.

On April 4, 1967, at the Riverside Church in Harlem, King gave testimony against the war in Vietnam belatedly (a full two years after a stinging denunciation of the war by SNCC's Robert Moses) but with deep self-criticism. His "Beyond Vietnam" address is a model of transformative organizing and evangelical discourse. "A time comes when silence is betrayal," he said, establishing his tactical objective to create a transformative moment in which forces in the church would be moved to actively intervene against the war in Vietnam.

He challenged himself to confront "the conformist thought within one's own bosom" and challenged the church to reject its embrace of a superficial patriotism and embrace the power of confronting one's own government. He condemned U.S. atrocities and humanized the so-called "enemy," the Vietnamese, as the United States dropped napalm and Agent Orange on civilian populations. He testified in support of the Vietnamese National Liberation Front (NLF) and their right to self-determination. Perhaps the most difficult but no less necessary task was to offer solidarity to the Vietnamese revolutionaries whom the U.S. government had designated as enemies. He laid the sources of the war directly at the feet of his own government, the United States. King understood the NLF as a legitimate resistance group and attacked their exclusion from all South Vietnam elections, which, he said, was justified by "myth and violence." He talked about learning from the heroic resistance of the Vietnamese freedom fighters, who he believed could offer encouragement to Black resistance movements in the United States.

King challenged those in power who had manipulated his belief in nonviolence to condemn the growing Black militancy in the country. In an observation that is one of the most influential of his legacy, he stated that there was no way he could be called upon to criticize anti-system violence in the Black community when his job was to challenge "the greatest purveyor of violence in the world today—my own government."

King, as an evangelist, called upon his audience to take a stand, to rise to its highest calling, to confront its own government, with all the risks that entailed. He called his troops into battle as a moral army confronting an immoral government.

He enumerated the crimes of his government, and humaniz[ed] and sympathized with the National Liberation Front, who[se] leaders he called his brothers. He still advocated his theo[ry] of militant, nonviolent direct action, but, with some sense [of] self-criticism as to the results of his own tactical plan agains[t] an immoral system, he validated the deep anger in the Blac[k] ghetto and offered his solidarity. He asked his audience to search inside themselves as he had, to take a stand, to decide: "Which side are you on?" And he asked them to come forth to his side. King was a great evangelist for the Movement.

Malcolm X was another great evangelist. One of his main objectives as an orator was to oppose what he felt was a shallow integrationism in which Black people were selling themselves short and Black establishment leaders were selling their people out. He wanted to generate a sense of Black identity, Black militancy, Black radicalism, tied to national liberation movements in the Third World.

When Malcolm X returned from his visits to Africa, having left the Nation of Islam, he formed the Organization of Afro-American Unity (OAAU). His focus had shifted—he wanted to place the "Black problem" in the United States in an international arena. Speaking to a multiracial audience at the Cornhill Methodist Church in Rochester, New York, on February 16, 1965, Malcolm proposed that Black people fight for both civil rights and human rights: "'Civil rights' are within the jurisdiction of the government where they are involved. But 'human rights' is part of the charter of the United Nations . . . [and its] Declaration of Human Rights. . . . [Y]ou can take your troubles to the World Court. You can take them before the world. And anybody anywhere on this earth can be your ally."

Malcolm assured the audience, "I don't want you to think I'm teaching hate. I love everybody who loves me. But I sure don't love those who don't love me." In his last years, he wanted white supporters to work in white communities directly confronting racism and supporting the international claims of Blacks in the United States.

The Recruiter

The role of the recruiter is to reach new members, to involve them in the organization, to get them to stay, and, over time, to bring them into the leadership of the organization. If you ask people how they first joined an organization, they will point to a speech or a book that changed their mind, an experience that etched itself into their brain, and an organizer who convinced them to get involved.

In my case, so many recruiters have taught me how to recruit. My political journey was influenced by many heroic acts, persuasive speeches, books, and films. I was deeply moved by the courage of the North Carolina A&T students and the martyred civil rights workers Mickey Schwerner, Andrew Goodman, and James Chaney. I was recruited to CORE by Lou Smith and Joyce Ware and sustained by George Wiley. I was recruited to the Newark Community Union Project by Tom Hayden and Bessie Smith. I was recruited to Students for a Democratic Society (SDS) by Paul Potter, Karen Ashley, Walter Lively, Kim Moody, and Bob Moore. I was recruited to the New Directions Movement in the United Auto Workers (UAW) by Jerry Tucker; and to the national environmental justice movement by Barry Commoner, Tony Mazzochi, Bob Bullard, Cynthia Hamilton, and Richard Moore.

In turn, I have recruited thousands of people to the movement through my public speeches, articles, and books; through my leadership of popular struggles; through direct one-on-one conversations; and because for forty-five years I have always been a member of an organization to which I was recruiting people. The recruiter has to have a lot of will and skill. It takes many individual conversations to attract the relatively small number of people who can convert their generalized anger into organizational involvement.

The Bus Riders Union recruitment model

At the Bus Riders Union, out of every hundred people we meet out on the buses, perhaps ten if the organizer is very good, become "dollar members" on the spot—they pay at least $1, get a temporary membership card, and are encouraged to attend the next general membership meeting. It is essential that money changes hands because money is a form of power and a reflection of real intent. If a person will not contribute at least $1 to support the work of the organization, there is less chance that he or she will show up for a general membership meeting.

Out of those ten "dollar members," perhaps three will decide to attend a monthly BRU meeting or come by the office to see a screening of the documentary film *Bus Riders Union*, by cinematographer Haskell Wexler. The organizers present the politics of the BRU based on our mission statement and principles of unity, and engage the new contact in a conversation. The entire new member orientation is based on the theory of transformative organizing. We explain that we pay great attention to conditions on the bus. We work for lower bus fares, clean-fuel buses, virtually no one standing, and doubling the Los Angeles Metropolitan Transportation Authority (MTA) bus fleet to create a 24/7 bus system. We see this as fighting transit racism and have won more than $3 billion in improvements—2,500 compressed natural gas (CNG) buses, lower bus fares, and more frequent service. This was followed by another major victory, a Bus Only Lanes Project on Wilshire Boulevard in which cars will be prohibited from driving in the outside lane during rush hours to dramatically speed up bus transit. After all, we are a Bus Riders Union, and we know most people come in the door to talk about conditions on the bus.

We then explain that the Bus Riders Union is a civil rights organization that also marches against the wars in Iraq and Afghanistan. We campaigned actively through our Take the Initiative Campaign to defend gay marriage and a minor woman's right to abortion without parental consent, and to oppose political initiatives that propose longer sentences, more police, more prisons. We explain our work as part of a larger strategy of a broad-based, popular movement in the United States led by low-income Black, Latino, and Asian/Pacific Islander communities and from there reaching out to a broad multiclass, multiracial, multitendency united front.

The orientation is based on answering a series of straightforward questions: Where are you coming from and what are you looking for? Do you understand who we are? Do you agree with our politics? Do you know what you are joining? Is this the right organization for you? While we are aggressive recruiters, we never want someone to claim they were brought in under false pretenses. The clearer the person is from the outset about the politics, values, and strategy of the organization, the better the chance they will stay with the organization.

Out of the ten to twenty new recruits we get at every general membership meeting, five to ten will join the organization that day, and two or three will decide to become active members of the Bus Riders Union. In essence, we get three types of responses from the orientation: 1) "I came here to get better bus service, and while I appreciate you putting your cards on the table, this is not the right organization for me." 2) "I generally like the other issues you fight for; I don't agree with all of them, but you do such a good job fighting for bus riders I'm happy to join." 3) "This is just what I've been looking for. I hate the conditions on the bus, I want to change the whole country, and I'm ready to fight."

The three people who become active members are required to attend at least four meetings a year in order to vote in the BRU planning committee election and run for office. They testify at the MTA, march on City Hall, and go out on the buses to recruit new members. The "dollar members" we sign up on the bus remain as dues-paying members who encourage other riders to join. They expand our influence and name recognition so that the next time we go on the bus we get a warmer welcome. The on-the-bus supporters sign leaflets and, in the age of cell phones, call elected officials right on the spot to advance our demands.

The recruiter's job can be broken down into three interrelated roles: *the opener, the closer,* and *the retainer.* The opener is adept at initiating a conversation with people and making a good first impression for the organization. The opener's job is to listen carefully to identify high-potential recruits, engage in a serious conversation so that the person understands the goals and objectives of the organization, and get all the information for the follow-up call or meeting.

Each organizer has to find her own voice, her way of approaching a conversation. Many different approaches work. I encourage organizers to tell the person something very brief about the organization. Many organizers will raise logical and effective questions like, "Where do you work? What do you think about the conditions on the bus? Do you know about our organization?" All of those are part of the opening. But I often add a question that is not asked enough: "Have you ever been involved in a movement before?" There is an implied assumption among many organizers that the person you are talking to is new to politics, and you don't want to make the mistake of underestimating the consciousness and history of a real leader right in front of your eyes.

Other times, we listen to the person's moving life story and, after a significant period of listening and questioning, move to the challenge: "Based on the experiences you have described, do you feel you would like to do something about it in a way that can impact the Black community, Latinos, immigrants, women, all bus riders?" Often, we hear in response, "What makes you folks think we can really change anything?" We have to acknowledge that there are some mornings that we wake up asking the same question. We well understand the difficulty of changing the system. We see the great move to the right by both major parties. If an organizer has not thought about this question or does not acknowledge the validity of the person's concerns, most likely he is repressing his own doubts.

On the other hand, the best openers are genuinely optimistic and are clear on the strategy and the game plan. He would answer, "There is a lot to be hopeful about. The election of Obama involved millions of people, including me. Those millions of people are people we want to organize to the movement. And look at the bus we're both sitting on. This new CNG bus was won by us. The BRU got the MTA to buy these buses, so how can you give up hope when you're riding in one of the biggest civil rights victories in L.A. and the country? We are building a transformative movement to change the system. What do you think? Let me tell you more about the Bus Riders Union." Not every person you talk to will respond to this approach. *But even at the opening, the key to recruiting someone is to combine four elements: listen very carefully and let the person talk, show a deep concern about very specific conditions people face, present very concrete demands, and frame the conversation within an up-front worldview of those fights as part of a larger social transformation.*

The effective recruiter is a thoughtful and confident advocate for the organization's long-range strategy. In the case of the Bus Riders Union, we explain our verifiable track record of victories: a successful civil rights lawsuit against the MTA in which the courts appointed us "class representatives" for 500,000 daily bus riders; getting the MTA to replace 2,000 dilapidated diesel buses with 2,500 new CNG buses; and stopping the MTA from cutting 100,000 service hours. It is essential that a social movement can point to something big that it won and show a history of victories all over the world. It is also necessary to explain to people that we well understand this is an uphill battle, which is why the person we are talking to is so important. Getting them to join the organization is a victory. We also explain that one of our greatest organizing victories, turning out 1,500 people at a public hearing to oppose another MTA fare increase in 2007, still could not prevent them from raising the fares from $52 to $62 a month. There are victories and defeats in this movement, and we agree with the African revolutionary leader Amilcar Cabral, "Tell no lies and claim no easy victories."

Then, I encourage the organizers to put the challenge back to the bus riders: "Don't you get tired of hearing your own complaints day after day?" "What makes you think anything can change if you do nothing about it?" "What power do you have as an individual, what possible hope do you have if you are not part of an organization?" "I feel lucky to be part of the BRU and I'm offering you the chance to share that experience." At the Strategy Center, we train our organizers to be good openers through role-playing, on-the-bus observation, and the sum-up process that accompanies all of our work. The opener has to avoid speechifying, talking *at* people. But the opener must also avoid being too sympathetic a listener when the person goes on and on about their problems but indicates no real interest in joining an organization.

The best openers have a dynamic chemistry with the people. Some organizers are initially shy, some are somewhat academic, some are loud, some are a little preachy and speechy, but they all convey a contagious belief in the organization and its mission, as well as a true love of the people that comes from the heart and is felt by the next new member.

The closer is successful at getting a new contact to join the organization—to become an active member. The closer is strong at follow-up calls and home visits after the initial contact has been made. Often, the key is to get the person to express what is going on in her mind and to effectively address the underlying concerns that stand in the way of signing up.

The Watchdog

In 1991, the Strategy Center was opening up a new organizing project, the Watchdog, in Wilmington, California, in the heart of the harbor area ringed by oil refineries—Texaco, Arco, Ultramar, Shell. The air was so heavy it felt like you could touch it, with a toxic soup of chemicals that forced the local schools to have to close for "smog" days. Organizers Kikanza Ramsey, Lisa Durán, and Chris Mathis knocked on the doors of five hundred community residents to assess who wanted to take on the oil companies and demand dramatic reductions in their toxic emissions. They found a lot of people with health problems— rashes, nausea, headaches, asthma, emphysema, leukemia, cancer—who were directly impacted by refinery emissions, but many were wary of taking on the corporate giants.

Representing the Watchdog, I spoke at the South Coast Air Quality Management District (AQMD), calling on the agency to take a more aggressive role in regulating the oil companies. After I testified, I was approached by a Latino man who I will call Eduardo Fuentes. He said he shared my goals and was the president of Parents Against Pollution, in Wilmington, California. I asked him how many parents were in the group and he said, "One. Me." I had to admire that a person from a working-class Latino background would invent a new organization, travel to the unfriendly climes of a regional regulatory agency, and hold his own among powerful pro-corporate forces.

As a closer, my objective was to make the case that he and Parents Against Pollution would be strengthened by joining the Watchdog. We had already recruited a dozen members, had a full-time staff of three, and a long track record in taking on large corporations. My concern was that he might prefer to be in an organization of one, self-motivated but also self-absorbed.

We next met at his home in Wilmington. I showed him my book, *L.A.'s Lethal Air*, a high-design, sixty-four-page book with sharp graphics, full-color charts and graphs measuring chemical assaults, and compelling pictures of working people from throughout Los Angeles. It talked about class, race, and gender as "the hidden categories of public health." The book was a centerpiece of our organizing in Wilmington. Eduardo said he liked the book, but he was concerned that we were asking working people to pay its list price of fifteen dollars. I explained that the book cost us a lot to print, and that we were asking for a contribution of ten dollars for it in the community and would take less as long as some real money changed hands.

No matter how many efforts I made to address his concerns, he seemed unconvinced. We were building an organization to fight Texaco and he wanted to keep arguing about the price of a book? What was really on his mind?

Finally Eduardo asked, "Does the Watchdog picket oil refineries or organize sit-ins or boycotts?" I said, "Yes." He then explained that he had grown up in Guatemala and had seen the government, with the support of the U.S. Central Intelligence Agency, kidnap and kill indigenous peoples, union leaders, and revolutionaries. He also talked about the growing anti-immigrant movements in California and wondered if our plan to organize an immigrant-based movement would generate government repression. He said he agreed with our program but feared the consequences of being identified with it.

I told him I understood his concerns. We were well known for being tactically astute. We began by building a strong community base and did not confront corporate giants until we had strong community support, many allies, and a tactical plan that could win. We were aware that many of our present and future members would be undocumented and would take tactical precautions—such as making sure that any nonviolent civil disobedience, if needed, would only be carried out by people whose immigration status was in order—but we could not guarantee there would be no retaliation.

After a long pause, a pensive Eduardo said, "I have expressed my fears, but I want to join." Eduardo ended up playing a very important role in the early stages of the Watchdog and gave us a lot of credibility in the community that helped the group gain traction and more members.

What I learned once again from that experience is that a good closer has to be a good listener. By taking the time to really build trust with Eduardo, I had been able to get him to express his true concerns, was able to address them, and close the deal in a principled, above-board manner.

Lastly, *the retainer's* role is to keep people inside the organization, build their leadership capacities, and find a good fit between their skills and the right structures within the organization. The retainer listens to and empathizes with members when they bring up reasons—personal or family pressures—for not getting more involved, but also pushes them to make the organization their own—to stop viewing their relationship to the organization from an outside vantage point and realize they are really part of the organization.

A good retainer pays attention to the conditions of people's lives, their health, family, and finances, and at times has to be able to offer some concrete help—setting up referrals to government agencies, helping people fill out forms, translating documents, providing rides home or childcare for members, or sometimes getting some food or rent money to a member. On the other hand, sometimes the job of the retainer is to get the member to reject a "consumer's" view of the organization through which they approach every problem from their individual needs as an outside observer or critic. Sometimes the retainer's job is to reach a mutual assessment with the potential member that there is not a good fit between their concerns and the objectives of the organization, and the goal is to create a principled separation rather than continue to try to retain the member.

The biggest job of the retainer is to teach a new member how to function in an organization and how to thrive in an organizational culture. Sometimes new members act like they have invented organizing; they are arrogant and really don't respect what the organization has built. Others are too deferential; they in fact have insightful observations but think the organization doesn't want to hear them. The retainer is a relationship builder. She has the energy to involve a relatively large number of members. She helps brings out the best in people. The retainer is also a mediator between the needs of the organization and the needs of new members in particular. She helps new members appreciate what the organization has achieved and how it has achieved it, while understanding that every new member is a potential source of innovation inside the organization whose opinions have to be cultivated and, many times, implemented.

Even the organizer with the most interpersonal and group-building skills will lose or retain people based on the level of political unity with the organization. A positive example of an effective retainer is Damon Azali-Rojas and his work with Patrisse Cullors in 2003. Damon, a lead organizer at the Strategy Center who was thirty at the time, was working with Patrisse, a gifted twenty-year-old organizer who had been with the organization for three years. Patrisse talked of how her first weeks with the organization made her want to be an organizer for her whole life. She still felt that way after two years, but, at the same time, as with all of us, there were ebbs and flows in her commitment. At the time, she was going through a particularly difficult period in her life—her father and brother were caught up in the prison system, and the family, financial, and school pressures were becoming overwhelming. Damon encouraged Patrisse to sit down with him and read *Towards a Program of Resistance,* a position paper written by some organizers at the Strategy Center. Damon said, "We went over it sentence by sentence, page by page." Patrisse said the study helped her find her bearings and raised her morale:

> I decided that even in the midst of my family problems, or even because of them, I was so angry at the system for what it was doing to my Black family, the constant police harassment, the criminaliza-

tion of my brother who has a medical, psychological condition. I realized what I had already understood. I need an organization, a center, to my life.

In 2006, Patrisse was twenty-three. She and Mark-Anthony Johnson—also twenty-three, and both graduates of our National School for Strategic Organizing—initiated the Summer Youth Organizing Academy to recruit and train a new generation of high school youth. Patrisse is one of the lead organizers of SYOA and teaches classes on political theory and organizing. She was recruited and retained through Damon's use of the Center's politics and his own initiative as a retainer. Now Patrisse carries out the same methodology to organize and retain high school youth. As she says, "Sometimes when the high school youth are feeling disoriented and depressed they say, 'I've got to get back to the Center.' They see the organization as helping to center them."

The best organizers are good openers, good closers, and good retainers. They get off to a good start and keep going throughout the organizing process.

The Group Builder

Recruiting brings individuals into the organization. Group building requires melding those individuals into committees, teams, and the other collective structures that carry out the organization's work. This is also when the new contact has to transition from joining the organization because of a specific organizer to meeting a lot of people in the group and wanting to be a team player. The group builder is a mentor and pays great attention to leadership development within the organization. The group builder focuses on creating forms of organization and healthy group dynamics that keep significant numbers of members engaged and committed.

When I worked with CORE, the first group builder I met was George Wiley. In 1965, George came in from Syracuse CORE, aided by his right-hand man Ed Day, to function as associate director of the national organization. George interviewed all the staff to come up with better operating procedures—regular staff meetings, work reports, lines of accountability. CORE had been the product of the more free-wheeling freedom movement culture where people made a lot of decisions on their own. We all had an assignment and knew how to carry it out, but with the exception of CORE's executive board, there was little collective decision making until George arrived.

One of the ways George worked as a group builder was to teach people, like me, how to operate effectively in an organization. In 1965, I was sent to Washington, D.C., as a CORE representative, along with Herbert Hill, the renowned labor chair of the NAACP, to meet with high-ranking officials of the Johnson administration's Department of Labor. The DOL was proposing a "summer work experience" for inner-city youth. The Pentagon had already initiated a "summer youth program" that sent Black kids to the front lines of Vietnam where they suffered astronomical casualties, so I was suspicious from the start.

This time, the administration proposed sending inner-city youth to agricultural work camps "to get job experience" where they would work side-by-side with migrant laborers, the most exploited and oppressed members of the workforce. While the DOL people assured us there would be worker protections, I told them I had worked for the National Sharecroppers Fund and knew that the migrant labor camps were one step above peonage and run with a whip hand by the agribusiness bosses. I said, "I think CORE will oppose the program but will of course bring back your proposal." I also came to understand (from undercover allies in the Department of Labor) that the inner-city youth were walking into intense labor unrest and would be unwittingly manipulated as strikebreakers to scab on Latinos and Pilipinos. I contacted Ralph Featherstone of the D.C. office of the Student Nonviolent Coordinating Committee, and we worked together to raise public challenges to the program.

When I came back to New York, I proposed that CORE launch a campaign to stop the project in its tracks. George Wiley agreed but challenged me as to my abstract moralism and absence of a tactical plan. He asked, "Do you know how the organization works, who makes the decisions, who has director James Farmer's ear? Have you thought about how you, as a new field secretary, can impact the organization's decision-making structure?"

Frankly, I had not asked myself any of those questions.

George, who supported my objectives, was my coach and mentor. He helped me move step-by-step, preparing my report, talking to other senior people, and finally getting my chance to bring my recommendations before CORE's executive board.

This was my first real engagement with James Farmer. I thought he would be thrilled at this investigative reporting, but he was immediately and decisively hostile to my proposal. Farmer explained that "his friend" Willard Wirtz, the secretary of labor, "would never do such a thing" and my information was wrong. He agreed that CORE would not participate in the program, but shut down my proposals for investigation into its abuses and organizing public opposition to the program. There was significant support for my proposal on the board, but, in the end, Farmer put his hand down very heavily and won the vote. I felt the disagreement was so significant that I considered quitting in protest, but George convinced me to stay. He argued that Farmer's too close relationship to the Democratic Party was not just in that instance. It was more structural. He proposed that we find ways to bring that debate into the organization in a constructive manner. He taught me, as I have had to learn over and over, that moral outrage absent of a plan is in fact adolescent, non-strategic, and counterproductive.

George Wiley, with his brilliant mind and ironic sense of humor, was a group builder. He later went on to help found the National Welfare Rights Organization. He trained people about the culture and procedures of an organization and how to be most effective in it.

A good group builder raises the performance of the entire group. Barbara Lott-Holland chairs the BRU planning committee. When Barbara tells folks that a five-minute bathroom break is five minutes, people scurry back to the meeting on time. She demands that the agendas are planned and the last week's minutes are ready for review. She reminds the group that there are back agenda items that have been tabled from week to week, and she pushes the group to stay up until midnight if necessary to catch up. She is very respectful of minority views and can often tell just from a member's body language that he is not comfortable with a decision—and she makes sure the person is encouraged to express his concerns and reservations. This is often to the benefit of the actual decision but always to the benefit of group cohesiveness. When presented with tactical forks in the road, she responds with thoughtful, engaging, and challenging questions. Once she is clear, she is inspiring; she argues strongly and persuasively for her views. She builds the planning committee as a decision-making body to bring out people's ideas, to mediate differences, to find compromises, to push ahead with a clear plan that over time "wins people over" and actually succeeds in the real world. She is a ferocious negotiator with elected officials and does not feel or display a moment of self-effacement in their presence. This models behavior for the other members and staff who watch her in action. She is a good listener but always shapes the terms of the debate. All of these qualities give her the moral authority to lead in her role as a preeminent group builder.

In the end, group building focuses on all the aspects of how an organization can retain members. An organization that trains a coterie of effective group builders develops a strong human infrastructure and great member loyalty. These are the groups that are able to make and change history.

The Strategist

The strategist develops the long-term vision of the organization consistent with the long-term interests of the movement. By the nature of the job, they function collectively in leadership bodies—an executive board, a central committee, a planning committee, a long-term strategy committee. In any group, whether explicit or implicit, its organizing plan is based on a strategy, and the strategists are the shepherds of the plan for the organization.

Strategy is a long-range plan for accelerating the movement of contradictions among political forces to achieve the desired goal of transformation. Strategy has five components—analyze the overarching political and economic contradictions of the system in the period within which you are working; identify the political forces against whom you are bringing your demands; determine the strategic aim, the most fundamental objectives you are fighting for; determine how to align your main forces and your allies; and develop clear programmatic demands that can rally a long-term movement.

The key job of the strategist, as an individual organizer, is to bring strategic thinking into every corner of an organization, so that both rookies and veterans are challenged to think about transformative objectives. That is why the lead strategists have to be the lead tacticians. If the strategy is to build a Black united front; a prosocialist Left; a multiracial, progressive LGBTQ movement; an anticorporate environmental movement; or a movement in support of Third World self-determination, then the strategy has to be clear to the people you are trying to organize. Keeping the whole chessboard in view, the strategist's job is to make sure the group does not lose sight of its broader political objectives.

Bill Fletcher and the Charleston Five

In 1967, when he was thirteen years old and living in Mount Vernon, New York, Bill Fletcher read the *Autobiography of Malcolm X*. It was a transformative experience that would shape his life choices. After that, he understood that "I needed to commit myself to Black Liberation and social justice and that meant doing something. Shortly thereafter I started reading about the Black Panther Party, and they seemed to represent what Malcolm advanced." Bill initiated the Black Student Alliance and Uhuru ("freedom" in Swahili) while still in high school—reflecting the Afrocentric influence on the Black movement at the time. He was accepted at Harvard but only made his decision to attend after witnessing on a site visit a demonstration at Massachusetts Hall by Harvard students. They were demanding that the university divest itself of Gulf Oil stock and protesting Gulf's ties to the brutal colonialist regime in Mozambique, while supporting self-determination for the southern African states of Mozambique, Angola, and South Africa. (One of the leaders of the demonstration was Randall Robinson, who later would write *The Debt: What America Owes to Blacks*.)

After graduation, Bill focused on working in the labor movement, taking jobs with the Postal Workers Union and Service Employees International Union, where he later became a special assistant to SEIU president Andy Stern.

In 1996, after years as a labor union activist and union

official, Bill was appointed the assistant to John Sweeney, the new president of the AFL-CIO. Bill's appointment was one reflection of the historic election in which Sweeney and the progressive wing of the AFL-CIO came to power on the platform of "organizing" and building the union back into a vehicle that would challenge big business.

In 2000, Bill helped lead the Charleston Five Case, one of the most high-profile U.S. labor struggles in the first decade of the twenty-first century. At that time, the International Longshoreman Association (ILA) Local 1422, a militant local of dockworkers in Charleston, South Carolina, was challenging Nordana, a Norwegian/Danish large-cargo shipping line. Nordana was trying to circumvent the union, refusing to pay prevailing wages or enforce strong health and safety provisions. It moved to hire nonunion workers, whose lower wages and lack of protection threatened the wages, livelihoods, and lives of ILA members—and the union itself. The ILA in the South is predominantly Black, and Local 1422 was and is led by its popular and independent president, Ken Riley.

The workers set up picket lines on the docks to discourage the use of nonunion labor, and at first the local police did not interfere. But on January 20, 2000, state attorney general Charles Condon, an antiunion government official, sent six hundred state troopers and highway patrolmen to break up the picketing. When some ILA members fought back to defend themselves, the police arrested five of them— Jason Edgerton, Elijah Ford Jr., Kenneth Jefferson, Ricky Simmons, and Peter Washington—to face felony riot charges with possible five-year sentences. The workers were put under house arrest that lasted more than eighteen months before their trial—able to go to work and union meetings but barred from any outside-family activities and electronically tied to their homes with ankle bracelets.

The workers welcomed Bill Fletcher as a valuable asset, and he immediately stepped up the strategic framing of the case. Instead of seeing it as yet another "good fight" that had to be fought, his goal was to make the Charleston Five Case a test case for the twenty-first-century civil rights and labor movements. In his words, "We have to make this the kind of issue the Scottsboro Boys were in the '30s, or that Huey Newton and Angela Davis were in the '60s. The state of South Carolina has declared war on labor and on Black workers in particular." Imagine the uphill battle. South Carolina was a "right to work" state or as the labor movement called it "right to work for less." It protected employers, advertised itself as a low-wage state to attract domestic and foreign investment, hated labor unions, and had a long history of racism against Black people. Under those circumstances, typical protests would not work, so what Bill proposed was a national and international campaign to paint South Carolina as a pariah, creating enough problems for the state's reputation and "economic climate" that it would decide to drop the charges. Even if that failed, the climate would become more favorable for the men if they had to go to trial. One tactical goal was to isolate Attorney General Condon so that other conservative forces would move against him in the larger interests of South Carolina's economic interests.

The local's president, Ken Riley, talked about the pivotal role that Bill played: "When Bill got involved, we saw what a strategist looked like. We saw what organization and discipline were really like." Bill helped them set up Charleston Five defense committees all over the country and in Europe as well. He had a long list of contacts and seemed to use every one of them for the cause. Bill asked Ken if he was willing to travel to get support, and Ken said "yes," figuring that meant once every few weeks. But as soon as he agreed, Ken was on the road four days a week. He and Bill set up a weekly conference call with defense committee members every Tuesday afternoon. Wherever any members of the team were, even when Ken was calling in from Europe, they all set their clocks to Eastern Standard time. "We all had the same strategy, but each had a different division of labor that Bill made sure we adhered to," Ken recalled. "When people could not do a job, Bill would say, quietly, 'I'll do that,' but when people did sign up for a job, it was understood you had no choice but to show up at the next conference call with the job done."

The campaign had an expansive tactical plan—letters to the governor; pressure on South Carolina corporations; a national AFL-CIO demonstration in Charleston of more than three thousand workers, one of the largest labor demonstrations in South Carolina history; and the establishment of Charleston Five defense committees in every city that was able to pressure their own elected officials to in turn pressure those in South Carolina.

Ken explained, "Bill taught us that as a strategist that you can't just 'do things,' no matter how creative, and expect to win. You have to go into a campaign against a far more powerful opponent with a clear, long-term strategy; a constantly evolving tactical plan; and a view from the beginning that the outcome is never in doubt—we will win the campaign no matter what it takes."

Eighteen months later, the Red Sea parted and the opposition split. Forces in the Republican Party were persuaded that the international campaign was hurting South Carolina and that Condon's efforts to describe the strikers as terrorists were causing more harm than good. Condon was taken off the case, and the charges were dropped. The Nordana Company dropped its plans for a nonunion workforce and allowed ILA Local 1442 members to unload their cargo. Under terrifying conditions, it is rare for a union campaign to win such an unequivocal victory.

With his experience in the civil rights and labor movements, and his greater study of strategy and tactics, Bill Fletcher gave a planned and conscious character to a campaign, and modeled the role of strategist. Through that process many of the brilliant worker-tacticians of Local 1422 learned how to become strategists themselves. He taught the workers to go beyond waging "the good fight" to organize a winning fight. Today Local 1422 is thriving. Ken Riley is a major figure in South Carolina civil rights and labor politics; and the victories of the case have strengthened the labor movement in South Carolina more than a decade later. This is the legacy of a successful strategist.

The Tactician

Where the successful organizer in the role of strategist must keep the organization on course, the organizer as tactician leads the struggle on the ground to carry out the objectives of the broader strategy. He analyzes the opponent's strengths, weaknesses, and game plan and anticipates the opponent's moves. Based on this assessment, the tactician coordinates and calibrates the maneuvers of the people's movement in order to maximize the advantage of surprise and mobility against a far more powerful opponent.

The tactician integrates all the research into plans for specific times, places, and conditions for action. She determines when to advance, when to retreat, when to focus on political education and when to send the troops into the field, when to unite with the mayor and when to take him on. Once deciding to take on the mayor, for example, she determines how to navigate a complex tactical plan to find the key demands, the correct approach, the appropriate tone, and the effective leverage to get him to change his mind and change his vote.

Tactics are all the forms of struggle and forms of organization— from big to very small—that are required to carry out the strategy. Generally a flyer, a rally, or a press conference is considered a tactic. But a sustained campaign is also a tactic. Creating a new committee within your organization is a tactic. Engaging members of Congress in conversation at a particular moment is a tactic. Let's look at major tactics, which I call "macro tactics," that are often so large and significant that they are confused with strategy.

In the famous Montgomery bus boycott, few understand that Rosa Parks was not just a historically pivotal protestor but an experienced tactician. On December 1, 1955, Rosa Parks refused to give up her seat for a white man on a Birmingham bus, an event that shook the world. What is less known is that Ms. Parks was not a random bus rider who carried out an individual act of courage. She was a conscious, transformative organizer and tactician who had been trained in the Civil Rights Movement with the NAACP—fighting debt peonage and lynchings. She had gone to meetings at the Highlander Folk School in Tennessee. Her refusal to give up her seat was a tactic in the larger strategy of the fight for racial equality.

A tactic can be an entire campaign. It can be an investigation into a particular problem in the community, such as Black residents' attitudes towards gangs and police brutality, or a demonstration to pressure elected officials and solidify your base of support. It can be an e-organizing campaign, in which organizational reporters cover the grassroots action in the streets, take pictures and write text, put it up on the website, then develop an e-mail blast to a growing number of supporters. Then they put the content up on Facebook and YouTube, and then go back to the e-mails to encourage people to put the material on their Facebook pages and, of course, go from e-action to street action by joining the next demonstration or rally, or just coming to a membership meeting. On the streets and the buses, organizers are able to get contacts to take out their cell phones and call or text an elected official on the spot—something unimaginable as a tactic just a decade ago. In grassroots election campaigns, e-organizing can get people to contribute online, sign up to join work teams, and, most importantly, volunteer to go door-to-door and phone bank to turn out the vote. E-organizing can never be the central tactic—the class war must be fought on the ground, not in cyberspace—but it is now a critical method by which to reach your base and the media and is an essential tactic in the organizer's arsenal.

Many do not realize how complex and diverse tactics are. The conversations an organizer has with members to build leadership and loyalty are tactics, as is the designing of a leaflet and the creation of a new form of organization such as a late-night street agitprops committee, whose members are willing to be arrested and whose skill, dexterity, and guts minimize the chances of being caught. The most effective tacticians have an organizing plan so that these moves are sequenced in a critical path to win specific victories.

Manuel Criollo

Manuel Criollo, the director of organizing of the Strategy Center, is a good tactician. As I said, your main strategists are the best tacticians because they know the long-term plan and can make day-to-day decisions to serve that objective. Manuel grew up in a Salvadorean working-class family; his stepfather was an industrial worker and his mother a domestic worker. Manuel went to University of California at Santa Barbara, where he majored in Chicano and Latin American studies, and came to the center after years working in community clinics.

As the director of organizing, Manuel has oversight responsibilities for all of the center's campaigns but mainly for the work of the Bus Riders Union and the Community Rights campaign. In the morning he checks the flyers going out on the buses and high schools for both campaigns to see if they contain a consistent antiracist message, even though one flyer is dealing with conditions on the bus and the other with the pre-prisoning of high school youth.

He meets with individual organizers before they go out, asking them: "Do you know your assignment?"; "Do you have any questions?"; "What are your priorities?" Then, while the young organizers are out in the field, he writes letters to government agencies, meets with coalitional partners, and participates in national social justice meetings.

A good tactician means going beyond being a person with a well-organized "to do" list. It means the ordering and sequencing of tasks, the combining of forms of organization and forms of struggle, with the goal of winning specific objectives—in this case, more members for the campaigns and, when possible, changes in social policy. That is the terrain of the tactician. Let's look at an example of how Manuel organizes and sequences some of the tasks.

We begin with a problem. The city of Los Angeles has a daytime truancy law that considers children who are late for school, even if they are on their way to school, to be truant. But it criminalizes that problem by having police handcuff students on their way to school or, often, right in front of their school, and serve them with summonses that require a court appearance and a $250 fine, something no low-income family can afford. This leads to large numbers of children in the Los Angeles high schools involved in the "school-to-prison pipeline" for doing nothing that should be a criminal act. And yet, in 2009, the Los Angeles School Police Department and Los Angeles Police Department arrested and detained more than 15,000 students who were on their way to school—in a school district of 650,000 students. For us, we also call it the "pre-prisoning of inner city youth," as the schools themselves take on the character of jails.

The first task in the Strategy Center's sequencing of tactics is to organize a strategy group to spend as long as a year investigating the actual conditions in the field. This involves formal education, like reading Ruth Gilmore's *Golden Gulag*, about the California prisons; meeting with Los Angeles Unified School District (LAUSD) board members, teachers, and students; and trying to assess the actual seriousness of the problem by doing questionnaires—after all, how serious is this problem and how passionately do people want to solve it?

As our student organizers hand out incident forms in the high schools, students write heart-rending stories of being cuffed, pushed around, and having their families have to raise $250 just because they were late to school—it makes you want to stay home. Often, the tardiness problem was because of delays on MTA buses or the normal problems of a low-income family trying to get so many kids out the door on time. Then, Manuel meets with LAUSD board members to see if they are upset about the idea of using police methods to deal with a normal problem of schools, students being tardy. He receives a positive reception from board members Monica Garcia, Steve Zimmer, and Nury Martinez, who encourage him and us to come back with alternative disciplinary ideas. Manuel then works with the Community Rights Campaign to generate a position paper—"Ticketing Toward Prison, and the Problems of the Daytime Curfew Law"—to make the case more effectively, which they can present to board members, teachers, students, and the media.

As a lead tactician, Manuel, as well as the group, makes an assessment—the problem is serious and widespread; we know what we are talking about—the students are concerned and angry, there are board members who are sympathetic, and there is a chance to change the policy.

Then Manuel and the group—Barbara Lott-Holland, Lizette Lazo, Andrew Terranova, Alejandra Lemus, Kendra Williby, Ashley Franklin, Damon Azali-Rojas—divide up the responsibilities and report out to the center every week. It's agreed that the group should approach the Los Angeles School Police Department (LASPD) and talk to the new chief, Steve Zipperman. Manuel leads the delegation, along with members of the Community Rights Campaign and the Dignity in Schools Coalition and board member Monica Garcia.

We ask Chief Zipperman to keep the promise of the recent change of policy, in which the LASPD has stopped making truancy sweeps and the ticketing of high school students inside the schools. We ask how they view the problem and see if there is any possibility of negotiating a solution. But why would the LASPD want to meet with the Community Rights group? Because we have a history of building a base, preparing our issues, and coming to negotiate from a position of some moral and political strength but also a belief that some changes can and should be made. And because we have the support of several school board members, the LASPD is more apt to agree to see us.

LASPD chief Zipperman says that he agrees students should not be ticketed and the police should exercise great restraint, because he does not believe in criminalizing truancy. All parties agree to meet again and hammer out some concrete language to codify the policy. Then, Manuel does what he does best. He sets up meetings with school board members, telling them the encouraging news from the LASPD. He meets with City Councilor Tony Cardenas to challenge the regulation that created the truancy tickets in the first place. Cardenas is open to changing the provisions of tardiness being an arrestable infraction and agrees that the $250 fines are punitive to the poor. A big tactic in getting city council interest was a report the Strategy Center produced showing Los Angeles Police Department (LAPD) ticketing information and putting it on a map of L.A. City with every high school highlighted by city council districts. That opened up city council members asking LAPD to provide information to the public that they had not provided.

Then, in April 2011, a major breakthrough took place. The Los Angeles Police Department and its chief, Charlie Beck, agreed to stop ticketing tardy students who are on their way to school. As the *Los Angeles Times* explained,

> Under new and "clarified" procedures agreed to by the LAPD at the request of advocates for students, truancy sweeps will no longer occur during the first hour of classes. And daytime curfew sweeps cannot be conducted except in response to suspected criminal activity by youths in the sweep area. . . . "It is not our intention to target our youths or to place undue bur-

dens on their families," said Chief Charlie Beck. "It's teachers, parents and students who will ultimately change the culture of a school," said Manuel Criollo, lead organizer for the Community Rights Campaign, which has long focused on this issue.

This work was carried out in collaboration with allies from the American Civil Liberties Union of Southern California and Public Counsel. This is one of the first times in recent Los Angeles history where a grassroots campaign has so fundamentally changed police policy—and begun to dismantle, one bar at a time, the school-to-prison pipeline.

For such victories to be possible it requires a lead tactician, like Manuel, who knows where the campaign is going: the strategist, to hold the group together; the group builder, to build a strong base; the foot soldier, who never walks alone. Manuel is also a good self-manager and can complete the whole task from start to finish.

The hardest job of any organizer is to train others—to teach the new organizers in training to be good tacticians at their own level of work, to keep in touch with the students, to come up with creative ways of keeping them involved, to elicit their enthusiasm and creativity, to study so you can testify in front of a city council or L.A. Unified School District board meeting. We encourage young organizers not to just show up at meetings but to come prepared with new ideas and innovations to keep the dynamics of the campaign moving forward. The best tacticians, like Manuel Criollo, are the ones who train other leaders; they demystify their knowledge and spread it throughout the organization.

The Communicator

The job of the organizer is to live in the world of language— a leader of the spoken and written word, an artist who can draw word pictures, inspire the imagination, make the struggle come to life. In social movements around the world, organizers move their audiences in different languages. And in a multilingual world, our movements and organizations are increasingly multilingual.

In South Africa, for example, the African National Congress organized a revolution by uniting the Black majority that spoke Ndebele, Xhosa, Zulu, Pedi, Sotho, Tswana, Swazi, Venda, Tsonga, as well as English and Afrikaans. Their Freedom Charter called for equality of languages, and their constitution now guarantees equal status to eleven official languages,

The Zapatistas in the Chiapas region of Mexico organize in Tsotsil, Tseltal, Ch'ol, and Nahuatl, among other languages, building their organizational infrastructure to enable equal participation of different language groups. In Bolivia, where struggles of the Indigenous peoples are central to the project of true, national liberation, the government of president Evo Morales, an Indigenous trade union leader, has worked to make Spanish, Quechua, and Aymara official languages.

President Hugo Chavez's fall 2010 tricontinental tour was extensively covered in *Correo del Orinoco International,* and, fortunately for English readers, editor Eva Golinger publishes an English edition. The planning for the World Social Forum in Dakar, Senegal, in February 2011, took place in English, French, Portuguese, Spanish, and Arabic.

In the United States, great organizers must be great linguists. When I talk about "the multinational working class," it is because in every major urban center the success of the movement involves uniting Nigerians and Koreans, Mexicans and Vietnamese, Dominicans, Blacks and Pilipinos. There are so many languages and cultures, so many ideas that have to come to life in so many dialects. Los Angeles claims 224 languages, not counting dialects, with 92 languages spoken by students in the Los Angeles Unified School District. The agitators and political educators, the strategists and tacticians, the foot soldiers and group builders—*they all need to have the consciousness that people think and dream in their native language.* It is the creative linguist who can find the beauty in the language of the revolution and make it come alive, can find the beauty in the people she is trying to organize, can find an original, compelling voice, can communicate in her native language and across languages. An organizer who is not bilingual or multilingual must, nevertheless, make the facilitation of languages central to her work.

In our growing multicultural world of organizing, there are organizations like Causa Justa::Just Cause, whose primary communication is in Spanish, and the Koreatown Immigrant Workers Alliance, whose primary language is Korean but which organizes workers in Spanish, Tagalog, Mandarin, and Malay. There is no urban setting in which "English only" is ethically or politically possible.

At the Strategy Center, we have built a trilingual organization with much of the work carried out in English, Spanish, and Korean. Early on, Lian Hurst Mann launched our fully bilingual publication, *AhoraNow.* After the first issue of *AhoraNow* came out, it received a particularly enthusiastic response from Spanish-speaking members, many of whom immigrated from Mexico, El Salvador, Nicaragua, and Guatemala. They were thrilled that their own organization had a political journal in their native language, but they also said that the Spanish, while good, was not excellent, and made many suggestions about areas of improvement. They embraced the challenge that Spanish is not the same for Mexicans and Guatemaltecas, Nicaragüenses, and Salvadoreñas; certain words and phrases are country specific.

One breakthrough moment came when a monolingual Spanish reader said, "¿Por qué dice que el movimiento está dirigido por los Negros? ¿No hay Latinos también en el liderazgo?" ("Why do you say the movement is led by Blacks? Aren't Latinos also in the leadership?") Everyone knows that the alliance between Blacks and Latinos is central to our strategy. *AhoraNow* had translated the collective expression "people of color" as *gente de color,* a phrase that many U.S. Chicanos use in political parlance. The monolingual Spanish-speaking member replied, finally understanding the problem: "En México y América Latina, 'gente de color' significa la gente negra." ("In Mexico and Latin America, 'people of color' means Black people.") In all aspects of organizing, it is often our mistakes that create the most indelible object lessons. From that time on, we understood collectively that communication across languages is not a transparent practice but is always a matter of interpretation (whether spoken or written) and always carries a cultural and political perspective. Lian commissioned many articles to be written in Spanish and "interpreted" in English, and always gave a byline to the "translator." The task for a successful organizer is to grasp and then teach that the voices of social movements and of ideology itself originate within specific languages of different nationalities and then are "interpreted" when spoken or written to communicate to others.

Once it faces the challenges of translation, every multilingual organization desires a culture in which people who speak different languages can participate democratically at the same time in the same space. While this is still a tremendous challenge, organizations like the Strategy Center approach this with the excitement inherent in still-difficult simultaneous interpretation. Rosa Miranda, Bus Riders Union member and organizer, says, "I thought, 'I will go to this meeting, but I don't know if I will understand what's going on.' When I arrived, they gave me the translation equipment, and I thought, 'Okay, at least I'm going to understand part of what they are going to say.' But then someone spoke in English and automatically it was translated into Spanish. When someone spoke Korean, automatically it was translated into English and Spanish. There is no language barrier."

Our practice has shown us that once people experience this equality in the course of struggle in a significant campaign, they begin to feel that they understand each other. Grandma Hee Pok Kim of the Bus Riders Union expresses it this way: "When I came here from Korea, I was like everyone else. I'd say, 'We're Korean. And they're Latino. And they're Black.' Since I came to the BRU, my mind has changed completely. You should see us when we go on a march."

The translators and interpreters move across cultural canyons to help build a multinational, multiracial, multilingual movement. The movement needs an army of linguists, interpreters, and translators who speak several languages fluently, who study the nature and structure of human speech, the different regional and national variations. We need organizers capable of simultaneous interpretation from one language into another who explain the meaning or significance of political expressions, express in different words, paraphrase, change from one form, function, state to another. In today's world, these communicators are critical to the international transformative strategy.

The Political Educator

A political educator is a storyteller who conveys the master narrative of the organization and the movement. She explains the whole picture, the long-range view that allows other organizers to situate their work in a broader historical, economic, cultural, and political context. The political educator presents a coherent ideological frame that gives confidence and a sense of orientation to the people she is organizing.

When I first joined the Civil Rights Movement in 1964, it was a time of passionate debates about politics. Everyone was trying to figure out their worldview, and events and consciousness were moving at warp speed. Tens of thousands of "Movement people" stayed up nights debating the great questions of our time: Was the system inherently racist and could it be changed? Why was the United States in Vietnam, and was the system imperialist? Could the Democratic Party be reformed or radicalized? Was a revolution necessary and was it possible? We read books, listened to speeches, engaged in long and heated political conversations. We all saw ourselves as political educators—presenting complex ideas that reflect a coherent worldview based on analysis and strategy that are used to convince, inspire, and recruit people to the movement.

Today, we need organizers who are effective political educators, who can put forth complex, controversial, and compelling ideas to working people and are willing to integrate talking about "the issue at hand" with talking about the system and how to change it. The effective political educator must go beyond a critique of the system to address questions of strategy and tactics, to be able to convince others that their organization and the movement has a real plan to win. The effective political educator must have an explanation of how the system works and a vision of how change can occur in the present that is exciting enough to make people want to get involved, to take risks, to think that some kind of structural change is possible and that a social revolution, even if decades or centuries in the making, is worth fighting for now.

Robin D. G. Kelley: Historian of peoples' resistance movements

Robin D. G. Kelley is a movement organizer situated as a college professor. He has taught at Emory University, the University of Michigan, New York University, Columbia University, Oxford University, and the University of Southern California, and is the author of *Hammer and Hoe, Race Rebels, Yo' Mama's DisFunktional!, Freedom Dreams, Thelonious Monk: The Life and Times of an American Original,* and many other books. As a political educator for the movement, Robin works to bring an integrated set of ideas that challenge the system itself, ideas that help and influence those working on the front lines.

He was born in 1962 in Harlem at a moment in history in which questions about the system filled the learning environments for many a future organizer. He went to P.S. 28 on 155th and St. Nicholas, at the top of Sugar Hill, for elementary school. As he explains,

> This was a period where you can't walk down the street without seeing people selling Mao's Little Red Books. There's a Black Panther Party presence. There was a Young Lords presence. I mean, every single

revolutionary organization existed in the streets and surrounded us. At my elementary school, we had the red, black, and green Black Nationalist flag, and we didn't think anything of it. The things I remember even more clearly were the nightly demonstrations at my elementary school to protest the conditions of the school. I went to school where the classrooms designed for twenty-eight students were holding as many as fifty, and I just remember the first slogan, as we picketed outside the school, was "Overcrowded, overcrowded," and we were like six, seven, eight years old. So that was the world that I felt nurtured me.

Movement organizations often ask a professor to explain complex ideas and events like the history of Black rebellion, feminist theory, or the history of U.S. interventions in Latin America. Robin is one of a small group of faculty who not only can teach those things but whose main subject of research and teaching is the history of radical social movements themselves. His teaching and research are also informed by a lifetime of practice.

In college, he got involved in Central American solidarity work, supporting the sanctuary movement and the liberation struggles in El Salvador and Nicaragua, and defending the sovereignty of Granada—a Black state in the Caribbean that was invaded by the United States and stays under U.S. control to this day. In 1984, he became involved with the Jesse Jackson Rainbow Coalition campaign and continued his journey in exploring Black liberation and social transformation for all people.

At the University of Michigan, Robin joined a group of graduate students who were organizing on behalf of teaching assistants but also doing serious organizing work with the Homeless Action Committee in Ann Arbor, fighting gentrification by the university itself. His teaching extends beyond the classroom, and, at the time, he gave as many as sixty talks a year to grassroots groups, passing along the lessons of Black

and progressive struggles to help them gain a broader perspective on their work. Moving back and forth from teacher to
student, he rolls up his sleeves and gets involved in the very
work he studies.

Robin Kelley's body of work focuses on several interrelated themes that the system has made a conscious effort
to suppress: he popularizes the rich history of a Black Left
that spans Black independent revolutionary, feminist, and
multiracial socialist thought. They were essential to the historic challenges to racism, such as ending Jim Crow and de
facto segregation, and the election of the first Black president,
Barack Obama. He situates himself in the tradition of transformative organizing, which seeks to transform the system
as a whole. He has modeled the activist role in the university. He argues that college faculty and students should become affiliated and engaged intellectuals. Students can study
Black Movements in the U.S., and also create their own role in
making social change by placing transformative organizing at
the center of their theory and practice—from challenging the
power relationships at their own university to working with
grassroots groups as part of their study. Robin describes his
role this way:

As a historian, I have to keep emphasizing that change
is never really evolutionary. It really is revolutionary.
It erupts at times when you least expect it, and yet
when you look at it in hindsight, it was there in the organizing work that preceded it. The sit-in movements
were not just accidental. It took years of organizing
from veterans coming back from the war to struggles
against anticommunism to hard organizing work in
churches, universities, factories, and plantations. In
terms of my own work, it's making sure that we as
a group don't get demoralized, that we keep talking
about that eruption. I also remind myself that one of
my goals in teaching courses like Black Movements
in the U.S. is to give students an alternative explana-

tion of how society is really changed by radical social movements, not primarily through electoral politics, because a lot of them think that's all there is. In fact, they often think that presidential electoral politics is all there is.

One example of Robin's use of different pedagogies to effectively teach the big picture is the use of "wiki organizing" to tap the organizing potential of the World Wide Web to aid grassroots groups and to get his students to do socially valuable work. The first big success was in 2005 when his students at Columbia worked with the Harlem Tenants Council to set up a website. Recently, eighty students in his Black Movements in the U.S. course have developed the content of a collaborative website about key social justice movements in the United States.

Robin Kelley is a dedicated political educator working closely with movement groups and challenging his students. He has a movement attitude as both an expert on the historic role of social movements and a participant in their very creation. Robin works to break the "white-out" of this work, to popularize, valorize, and identify himself with the work of social justice, labor, feminist, and community groups that are doing important work in working-class communities of color and in prisons, sweatshops, and the fields. He is always asking the question, "How can I be of use to organizers?" and, even more unique, allowing the organizers to answer the question, saying, "This is the political education we need!"

The Agitator

The agitator is a political educator and mass mobilizer who focuses on a specific abuse of the system, generates insight and anger, raises people's consciousness against the system itself, and propels them into motion. The agitator speaks at a rally and gets the crowd fired up and ready to march on City Hall because of a government raid on undocumented workers or a police shooting of an unarmed Black man. A good march or demonstration raises agitation to an art form. At immigrant rights marches, T-shirts proclaim, "No Human Being Is Illegal," and "I didn't cross the border, the border crossed me." At anti–Iraq War marches, the agitation was about "No Blood for Oil." At pro-union demonstrations in Wisconsin in 2011, some carried signs reading "Unions: the People Who Brought You the Week-end."

The agitator builds on a powerful and shared experience, the charged moment when a group of people realize that a given outrage is part of an entire system gone wrong. The agitator propels a group of workers about to go on strike into consciousness and into motion. Where once the people suppressed their anger or felt resistance was futile, now they want to act. They want to join the movement; they want to make the system pay.

The agitator mobilizes a crowd to demand that a racist policeman be arrested and also that the entire police force is placed under civilian trusteeship. They want Texaco to stop polluting. They want auto-free zones. They want "1,000 more buses and 1,000 less police." They want all raids on undocumented workers stopped immediately. They want all U.S. troops out of Afghanistan, Iraq, and Pakistan. The agitator is on the front lines of the action and is moving people to understand the system itself and to take action.

Every meeting, rally, direct action—each situation is different and dynamic. A good agitator is well prepared. He knows the strategy, understands the overall tactical plan, knows the "end game," but will make specific moves based on "time, place, and conditions." He thrives in the rapidly moving field of events, when the masses are in motion and the power structure is on the defensive. He can sense openings and must be able to exploit them.

The agitator gets right to the point, thinks creatively, and has a good sense of sarcasm and humor. She has to think on her feet and cannot rely on mechanical, stale, or rehearsed material to make the connection from the specific problem to a broader outrage against the system to a concrete demand.

Agitation has been a great strength of Bus Riders Union organizers and members. In 1996, Kikanza Ramsey, an organizer for the Bus Riders Union and a leader in the "No Seat, No Fare" campaign, went on a Metropolitan Transportation Authority (MTA) bus on Crenshaw Boulevard in Los Angeles and spoke to a captive audience of forty people sitting and another thirty people standing. She told the bus riders:

> Look at these overcrowded conditions right in front of your face. This is a separate and unequal bus system. This is what transit racism looks like. The MTA subsidizes the whiter, more suburban rail system by raiding funds from our bus system. That is why the buses are overcrowded. The MTA does not care about Black and Latino people, does not care if you are late to work. Does not care that you are squashed in this

bus like sardines. That is why our poster says, "No somos sardinas." We are not sardines. That is why we are calling for a No Seat, No Fare campaign. We are asking you to refuse to pay your bus fare and just walk past the fare box. Don't pay for racism.

From that one brief but riveting agitational intervention, we would hear bus riders say back to us, to their coworkers, to their families: "This is what racism looks like," "No somas sardinas" ("We are not sardines"), "No Seat, No Fare," "Don't Pay for Racism." These were agitational slogans that could capture an entire criticism of the system or call to action in one phrase, slogans that would drive people to righteous anger against the system, agitational slogans that would propel people into action. Tens of thousands of bus riders in the next month refused to pay their fare. The drivers union defended the strike. Some, citing their contract in which they are obligated only to "quote the fare," did not enforce it. Some bus drivers, especially the Black, Latino, and women drivers told the passengers, "Support the Bus Riders Union. Just walk on by," and they put their hands over the fare box. Through our agitation, we had turned the buses into "a moving site of contestation," as historian Robin D. G. Kelley described our work.

In 2007, the MTA moved to raise the price of the monthly bus pass from $52 to $62. The BRU militantly opposed the fare increase and ran its most effective city-wide campaign. To blanket the city, we distributed a thousand lawn signs reading, "Mayor Villaraigosa: Stop the MTA's Racist Fare Hike," to pressure the mayor, with four seats on the MTA board, to take action. (Note: We did not say the mayor was racist; we said the MTA's fare hike was racist and that he should stop it.) We did a lot of on-the-bus agitation and received the endorsement of Spanish-language media, which covered our organizers on the evening news as if they were folk heroes. This organizing work generated the largest protest in the history of the MTA—1,500 people, 1,490 of whom were on the side of the BRU. Three hundred people testified, each given one minute. An angry Latina bus rider, holding her three-year-old son in her arms, told the board, "I do not have ten dollars a month for a fare increase. With three people using the bus in my family, we do not have thirty dollars a month for your fare increase. What do you want me to do? Take the clothes off his back or the food out of his mouth?"

Grandma Hee Pok Kim, a leader of the BRU, scolded the MTA in Korean with such fury the room was shaking: "You are violating our civil rights. You are attacking the people, the elderly, our children. You are heartless. You must vote no on the fare hike." Grandma Kim delivered her agitation with militancy, anger, and sarcasm. She enunciated every word and gave every punch line extra emphasis. She pointed her finger at those in power and reprimanded them for their abuses. She told a joke about them and laughed at it herself. Her audience, most of whom didn't speak Korean, hung on her every word. They were already cheering before they heard the translation, and they cheered again when they heard the wit and wisdom of her actual remarks translated.

Despite our efforts, a hard-hearted group of elected officials, almost all Democrats, voted to tax the poor to pay for their pork-barrel rail projects. The fare increase went into effect, and we were unable, even through perhaps our greatest organizing ever, to stop them. At that point, the BRU agitators were needed again. Their job was to raise the morale of the movement. They had to expose the abuses of the system so that those who had fought so hard would believe that their actions had historical significance and that the next battle in the longer war was worth fighting. It would take the political educators going back to the drawing board and having the heart-to-heart talks and sum-ups necessary to build on the work of the agitators and solidify the base.

In each case, the agitators understood that one of their goals was to influence people in power, but their primary audience was the oppressed, the movement. A successful agitator raises the morale and fighting capacity of her members. She contributes to high retention rates through the ups and down and victories and defeats of a long-term campaign.

The Fund-Raiser

The most successful organizers are successful fund-raisers. The revolution is not free of charge. At times, a group, at the outset, does not have an office and is staffed by volunteer members. When the organization has a strong strategy and tactical plan, it can generate high-visibility, high-results work. It also has to have the political understanding that fund-raising is a central task and develop organizers who fight to become good fund-raisers as part of their organizing work. Money can pay for a large and well-equipped office for an effective center of operations, food for meetings, an emergency fund for member needs: rallies, travel, legal bills, billboards, lawn signs, computers, website design and execution, member stipends, and staff salaries. Money is power—the power to carry out your work.

When the Strategy Center was in its incubation stage, I wrote a concept letter to Richard Grossman, a militant environmentalist who had written the book *Fear at Work*. Richard, along with the late Tony Mazzochi of the Oil, Chemical, and Atomic Workers Union, was organizing me to understand the urgency and strategic significance of environmentalism. I explained my vision of the Strategy Center as a left experiment, a new entry into the environmental movement with a strong base in the Black and Latino communities and the insurgent wing of the labor movement. Richard forwarded my letter to David Hunter, a well-known progressive philanthropist whom I had heard of for decades but had never met. David called me, "Is this Eric Mann? Come to New York, I want to talk about funding your work." I rushed to New York. David and I talked for several hours at the Penta Hotel across from Madison Square Garden. He put me through a rigorous interrogation about plans for the Strategy Center.

David asked, "If you focus on the Black community, how do you deal with white people? If you are independent of the Democratic Party, how do you work with progressive Democrats? Why do you think your experiment will get off the ground if you have no money and I am your first possible contributor? Why do you think you can raise money with such a working-class point of view?"

I answered every question in a straightforward manner. I had thought about every question he had raised, felt that those were the right questions to ask, and apparently gave him answers he felt were worth his investment. In two days, he raised the first $50,000 for the Strategy Center and told me, "Go pursue your dream."

What I got out of that experience is that fund-raising is political. You lay out your politics, your strategy, your goals and objectives, your demands, and your tactical plan and then ask people to give funds to you. They either will or they won't. If no one will support you financially, that may be information you want or need to hear. It doesn't automatically mean the project is not worthwhile, but if after many rejections and reformulations, you can't find people willing to give their own money to your organization, perhaps there is some need to go back to the drawing board.

Twenty years later, the Strategy Center has fifteen full-time staff, many interns, and hundreds of active members. The entire organization does fund-raising, with some people more motivated and skilled at it than others. Still, we must struggle harder so that *every* organizer, every member fund-raises more aggressively for their organization. In order to be a successful organizer, you have to be a successful fund-raiser. At the core of our appeal is the same approach with which we began: a firm, ethical, straightforward political approach to people and a firm rejection of any efforts to hide or distort our representation of ourselves in pursuit of money.

Cesar Chavez was a relentless fund-raiser. He taught his organizers the life and death importance of raising funds from the farmworkers, the poorest of the poor who made up the base of his organizing campaign. He explained,

> I would go door-to-door to talk to the *campesinos*. I explained that the dues for the United Farm Workers was $15 a year. I would ask the workers to contribute to the union organizing drive. One worker told me, "I am very poor. Can I have the dues for $5?" I replied, "Do you want one third of your liberation? Are you trying to build a union on sale? If I went into your house, would I find a six pack of beer or clothes worth more than $15? If you have money for that you must have money for the union—if you believe in it. Management is powerful, we must be powerful. The dues are $15, what do you want to do?"

At the Strategy Center, I use the Chavez story over and over to train organizers to be aggressive fund-raisers on the bus. I tell them, "The working class values money, and so do we. How can you sign up a member, when our dues are $10 to $50 a year, if you are afraid to ask for even a dollar? Let the bus riders show you if they think the organization is worth supporting or not." When an organizer is an aggressive fund-raiser, she conveys a sense of confidence in the organization and often generates a reciprocal response from a potential member. Often, people's first way of joining is to give money.

The Annual Political Party

At the Strategy Center's "Annual Political Party," our yearly political celebration, we have developed a theory of fund-raising: building a long-term family of supporters who come each year looking forward to the music, spoken word, agitational speeches, and the fund-raising appeal. In 2009, our twentieth year as an organization, we set our highest goal ever, at $30,000. At our 2009 twentieth-anniversary party, 350 people attended, of whom 25 percent were Black, 25 percent Latino, 15 percent Asian/Pacific Islander, and 35 percent white. The largest single group was high school and college students, but the audience ranged in age from sixteen to ninety-nine.

Barbara Lott-Holland, Tammy Bang Luu, and Martín Hernández, leaders of the center, roam the floor with microphones. When people contribute, they encourage them to testify. When there are pauses and silences as people figure out at what level they want to give, I wait quietly. I ask if someone in the audience could start the appeal with a contribution of $5,000. A generous donor contributes that sum. I ask, "Who wants to give between $1,000 and $4,999?" Seri Bryant, a longtime supporter, pledges $1,000. Kate Kinkade and Patrick Ramsey, the chair and secretary of the Strategy Center board, pledge their annual $1,000. Daniel Kim, Cheryl Higashida, Dan DiPasquo, and Elena Astilleros, supporters of the National School for Strategic Organizing, contribute $3,000 as a team. An anonymous donation moves us to $10,000 within the first minutes. We are on the way.

John Bell, a low-income bus rider, says, "I love the Bus Riders Union. I came in wanting to get better bus service, and now I have learned about civil rights and global warming." He pledges $250. Rosalio Mendiola, a BRU founder, pledges $150—out of his salary as a room service waiter. A boisterous group of Black and Latina students from Cleveland and Westchester high schools contribute $100, $200, and then $300 as each table competes with the others. Robert M. Taylor, a long-time BRU member, contributes $10 and gets a great round of applause.

I ask Kate Kinkade, who has been at every party since 1990 with a calculator as part of the ritual, "Kate, what is our number?" She says, "$15,500." The group is revved up; we are halfway there.

Finally, as we get to $28,000, people yell out, "Let's get to $30,000 so we can start the dancing." In the next few minutes, new contributions come forward. Kate announces the total: $30,775! The group erupts into applause. People hug each other. Every year people tell me, "I have never been to a party where so many people love to give money and actually look forward to the fund-raising appeal."

The funds we raise at the Political Party are a small part of our overall budget. But as an annual ritual, they give us the moral legitimacy to ask for significantly larger amounts of money from people with far more resources. Those who attend are deeply moved. They see 350 people invested in the success of the center, and the poorest of the poor give a very high percentage of their income to support the work they know is theirs. For funders looking to make larger investments, they recognize that a demonstrable grassroots funding base is a reflection of the solidity of the organization itself.

Of course, every successful fund-raiser seeks support from affluent allies. The late Don White, who spent decades as an organizer with the Committee in Solidarity with the People of El Salvador (CISPES), was a legendary fund-raiser. In *Compañero,* a film on his life by Peter Dudar and Sally Marr, Don recounted, "At many CISPES actions, we carried out civil disobedience leading to arrest. At one militant action, I ended up locked up in a jail cell with the actors Martin Sheen and Ed Asner and the musician Jackson Browne. I thought to myself, 'What a great opportunity. I have a captive audience with my major donors.'"

Historically, a successful movement requires most of its

donors (not most of its money) to come from the working classes. Movements of the poor are significantly funded by members of the middle and affluent classes who support their moral appeal. This has been a dependable model throughout history. In the building of a progressive movement, money is a critical component of power to the people.

The Comrade and Confidante

The comrade and confidante wins the respect and trust of the people, holds the organization together, counsels members and fellow organizers, and understands that the personal is political and the political is personal. After all is said and done, an organization rises or falls on the quality of the relationships at its core. Comradely relations built in the course of struggle strengthen the work and ensure the stability of the organization. You must feel that the people with whom you work the most closely literally have your back.

A classic example of such bonds was seen in 1990. Shortly after Nelson Mandela was released from prison in South Africa, he came to the United States on a national tour. At virtually every press conference, reporters combined adulation with challenge. Mandela was asked, "We are so proud of you, but how can you work with the South African Communist Party [SACP]? How could you appoint Joe Slovo, a communist, as minister of housing?" Mandela replied that the Mandela and Slovo families have been close friends during many decades of the struggle against apartheid, and that the South African masses have great respect for Joe Slovo.

Obviously the core of the African National Congress (ANC) was political, but often it was personal friendships that were the unbreakable cement of the movement. In the face of systematic police infiltration, being a trusted comrade and choosing your friends and confidantes wisely were a life-and-death part of the job.

The confidante is an essential role in a world that is not safe or trustworthy. In an organization, a leader who is trusted helps members address the contradictions in their own lives and their work. While I had understood this capacity in others as soon as I joined the movement, I saw this aspect of my own job dramatically expand when I was the coordinator of the UAW Campaign to Keep GM Van Nuys Open, from 1982 to 1988. I worked on the shop floor of a five-thousand-person assembly plant. I was given early recognition as a strategic and tactical leader, but over time many workers also saw me as someone they could talk to and confide in—a comrade.

Kelly Jenco talked to me about her years of spousal abuse and the critical role of Haven House, a home for battered women that saved her life and that of her children. She and I began to investigate the lives of the five hundred women who worked in the plant and were overwhelmed by how many women were experiencing battery and violence in their relationships. Many men were threatened that their girlfriends or wives had a better job than they did and worked in a factory with many men. Kelly, Dorothy Travis, and I set up the union's first Women's Committee and got our union local to make an annual, substantial contribution to Haven House.

Manuel Hurtado would talk to me about how angry he was, as a Mexican, about the anti-Mexican chauvinism of some Chicano workers—people of Mexican descent who have been in the United States for at least one generation. Manuel said, "They don't like when I speak Spanish, and then they say my English is no good. I tell them, 'What would you rather have? A shop steward who will fight for you who speaks Spanish and pretty good English, or a company man who sells you out in perfect English?'"

Manuel and I organized an in-plant movement for equality of language rights that involved the union's most progressive Chicanos, such as Mike Gomez, the head of the union's political action committee, and Black workers, led by Jake Flukers, a skilled tradesman from Louisiana. We got our local to institute Spanish translation and headphones at the union meetings and to carry out worker education on the contributions of Mexicans to the union movement.

Mark Masaoka, as one of few Japanese Americans in the plant, talked to me about the constant anti-Japanese comments he was receiving at work. General Motors management and the right wing of our union local led a campaign to blame declining auto sales and the problems in the plant on "unfair Japanese imports." Many workers were furious at the Japanese while docile towards GM management. Mark, our UAW Local 645 president, Pete Beltran, and I carried out political education in the plant to counter anti-Japanese xenophobia. We ridiculed the company mascot, a bear named BEBI (an acronym for Better Effort Beats Imports) that was used by management to encourage the workers to work even harder to save their own jobs. We challenged the workers to decide which side they were on: fighting the company or fighting the Japanese? Over time, through leaflets and hundreds of one-on-one conversations, we beat back the hysteria of the Toyota-bashing movement. We got many of the workers refocused on GM as the main adversary trying to close down our plant.

In each case, being a confidante involved having the trust of the workers. That trust made it possible to work together and challenge the ideologies of male chauvinism, spousal battery, "English only," racism, and xenophobia inside the workers movement. In each case, what began as a private conversation based on mutual trust was transformed into an organizing tactic to address the larger problem in which the personal problem was situated.

A few years later, I needed other workers to be my comrades and confidantes. In 1984, I badly injured my back on the assembly line and was out of work for four months. When I got released by the doctors to go back to work, my back was still hurting me. I was supposed to be put on "light duty" until I completely recovered. Fat chance. My committeeman, the union representative, was in the right-wing faction of the union and allowed, or even encouraged, management to put me on some of the hardest jobs, which made my back even worse. Every day was a struggle to go to work. I worried that the collaboration of the right wing of the union and the company would force me back out of work. One night I had to crawl up the stairs to my second-floor apartment at two in the morning after the shift was over.

After many workers came by my station to yell at my foreman, they organized a rank–and–file group who demanded that the foreman transfer me to a job I could do. After a brutal month on my original job, the sustained workers' support succeeded. I was finally transferred to a job that I could do without doubling over in pain. I owed it to the workers who were my friends and confidantes.

If you are indeed a trusted comrade, and a good leader, others will confide in you and fight to protect your leadership. They will bring you criticisms and insights, presented in a constructive manner, that are invaluable. No matter how self-critical and observant we are, there are many mistakes each of us makes in life that we cannot see or understand without the help of others. At the Strategy Center, I am fortunate to have close comrades who will take me aside, which I appreciate in itself, and explain to me things I have done that were arrogant, chauvinist, insensitive. They will point out ways I have been inconsistent and even vacillatory— changing my mind and contradicting something I said only a few days ago without realizing it. They show me instances when I did not listen to or respect the ideas of others and assumed I was right, when in fact they understood the situation far better than I did. Engaging me in a process of introspection and self-improvement, this network of close comrades and confidantes is my lifeline and a key to my successful leadership.

In unions and community groups, organizational politics are often treacherous. If people don't trust you, don't have your back, don't confide in you, you may never know of the plots, coups, and *movidas* that are all too frequent in political life. If they see you as a friend and confidante, they will warn you about conspiracies and intrigues and ally with you to root out the conspirators. No matter how astute you think you are, factionalism and duplicity are hard to uncover, since the best of your opponents are very good at disguising what they do. In the end, you have to make a calculated assessment of who you trust and who trusts you. If you choose wisely, you will succeed in your work. Being a comrade and confidante is crucial for the advanced stages of the group-building process and for protecting the leadership so that the organization can grow and survive.

The Cadre

Cadre are the most developed, committed, dedicated, organizers. Cadre are the backbone of the organization; together they form the skeletal structure around which a larger organization can be built.

In part 2, "16 Qualities of the Successful Organizer," I'll go into detail about the many qualities of the cadre. *But in terms of the job description, three critical elements of the cadre's role are 1) being willing to do whatever the organization asks; 2) bringing tremendous volunteerism to the job; 3) being capable of building a base and evolving a project, campaign, or organization.* Because many people who are organizers are now paid in that position, it's often difficult to assess if a person is cadre or an excellent employee. It is often among the unpaid, volunteer organizers that we can see what cadre really look like.

Throughout history, the term "cadre" has referred to the most gifted, professional organizers. The term "professional" in this context does not refer to people who are paid to do the job but rather to those who see fundamental change as their life's work. At the height of the Civil Rights Movement, the cadre who were the models of our times were the Freedom Riders of CORE and the field secretaries of SNCC. In Asia,

Africa, and Latin America, popular insurgencies were led by cadre who were part of national liberation organizations.

If there is to be a left turn in the future of the United States, it will require a geometric expansion of the number of dedicated cadre. In every successful mass movement, cadre have been the motor force of history rooted in actual struggles. In a movement of thousands, cadre will number in the hundreds. In a movement of millions, cadres will number in the tens of thousands. They wake up in the morning knowing they are in charge and ready to go into battle. They are responsible, respected, and have been given the moral authority by others to lead. They have been intensively trained and mentored, and they have developed skills and abilities through years of practice. As leaders, they work with less-developed or less-committed people in order to expand their development and commitment. In a democratic organization, the cadre insure the participation of all.

When the young kids went down South to risk their lives for civil rights, not all were cadre, but virtually all who stayed became so, for the cadre were the most dedicated. As they met the battle-hardened veterans of years of indigenous fights against the Klan, they were schooled and pushed. In 1960, Ella Baker suggested to Robert Moses that he visit Mississippi to see the possibility of direct-organizing work. Moses went to see Amzie Moore, the vice president of the NAACP, who had spent decades organizing chapters in the most Klan-infested areas of the state. Moses later recalled, as Charles M. Payne describes in *I've Got the Light of Freedom,*

> Amzie laid out what was to become the voter registration project of the Delta of Mississippi. He wanted SNCC to come and do it. In fact, he was the only person in the leadership of the NAACP I met at the time that was willing to welcome SNCC. I think he saw in the students what had been lacking—that is, some kind of deep commitment that no matter what the cost, people were going to get this done.

In the Mississippi Organizing Project, everyone involved, from the local residents to the students who were in the leadership of the project, was cadre: C.C. Bryant, E.W. Steptoe, Webb Owens, David Dennis, Emma Bell, Bobby Talbert, Ike Lewis, Marion Barry, Mary Diggs, Alice Blackwell, Laura McGhee, Ethel Brady, Pinkie Pilcher, Bob Zellner, Dottie Zellner, Stokely Carmichael. In fact, SNCC had the largest group of trained cadre I have ever seen with my own eyes—the list includes hundreds. Today, when the movement is not at the same level of dedication and the role of risk-taking is reduced (although those conditions are changing rapidly), we still see cadre in several contexts.

Andrew Terranova

When there are members who work so hard that people think they are on staff, Robby Rodriguez of the Southwest Organizing Project calls them "supermembers." Andrew Terranova is one example at the Strategy Center. He went through the National School for Strategic Organizing, went to the Bay Area to get his teaching credentials, and decided to come back to Los Angeles to work with the center as a volunteer. He got a job as a school teacher and works very long hours preparing lessons, grading papers. He often comes to Strategy Center meetings with great enthusiasm but sometimes has a tendency to doze off as the meetings grow later, for he has been up since 5:00 a.m. preparing for class. When Andy first applied to the National School, I told him that we had a racially diverse class that had already been selected. I encouraged him to apply for the next year. He said he would wait his turn. He spent the year working in New York with "Irish to Free Mumia Abu Jamal" and making a living as a carpenter. He was accepted into the school the following year, 2001. Today when I ask him to do a job, he sometimes indicates it isn't his favorite thing to do, but he will say, "But then, I'm cadre. I do what has to be done."

So, how do you get the qualities of dedication that fulfill

the job description of cadre? Are they innate? To some degree, yes, but everyone is trained through an organization. Everyone is organized by someone, and the great organizers have been trained and mentored by great organizers, great teachers. In the final analysis, it is a life choice. Out of that process, the organizer makes the decision to become a professional cadre, an agent of social change.

When most people first become politically involved, they begin as activists. The activist attends meetings, goes to marches, writes letters, and, after the organization develops confidence in her, might be encouraged to speak at an event. But she is still an activist—a good one, but not yet an organizer. The activist herself cannot come into being without an organization run by organizers—who have organized every event and action she participates in. When a group is fighting to win and is carrying out its work with a planned and conscious character to advance a long-term strategy, the most dedicated organizers, the cadre, are essential. Over time, with training, a strong class stand, close ties to the masses, and a willingness to learn, the activist can become an organizer, the organizer can become cadre.

For a successful movement organization, every meeting, every march, every campaign, every tactic is part of a campaign against a powerful adversary. To carry a campaign to victory, any serious organization must have a base that can force some institution to change. You cannot build such a base without an organizer; you cannot build a successful movement without cadre.

As the anthropologist Margaret Mead observed, "Never doubt that a small group of thoughtful, committed citizens can change the world. Indeed, it's the only thing that ever has." So, if you don't have cadre, you don't have a chance. But if you do have a small group of advanced, dedicated leaders, a core of cadre, your organization can grow exponentially and victory is possible.

PART 2

The Qualities
16 Qualities of the Successful Organizer

The great transformative organizers stood up to mighty systems of oppression and exploitation to lead mass movements for liberation. Their names are recognized world wide— Spartacus, Nat Turner, Harriet Tubman, John Brown, W.E.B. Du Bois, Mahatma Gandhi, Malcolm X, Martin Luther King Jr., Nelson Mandela, Fannie Lou Hamer, Hugo Chavez, Rigoberta Menchu, Yuri Kochiyama. They are known for their bold views, radical plans, and historic victories.

Transformative organizers are driven by an ideology and ethical vision of radical change and a daily practice of working with society's most exploited, oppressed—those most impacted by the crimes and punishments of the system. Your transition from critic to dedicated activist and transformative organizer can help make history in your own lifetime.

In "The Job Description: 12 Roles of the Successful Organizer," I explained the component parts of the job of a transformative organizer. The qualities that I present here are what make the difference between success and failure in the practice of each particular job role. Each quality is discussed separately because there are many areas of our work, and breaking each one out allows interrogation, evaluation, and rectification in the process of continuous improvement.

The qualities represent an integrated, qualitative way of looking at life, being, and acting. As you will see, many of these qualities are "clustered" and interact with each other. As I explain, the most successful organizer must be excellent in many of these qualities and at least pretty good in virtually all of them.

The qualities are best understood and learned one at a time. It has taken me decades to understand each one. A quality can best be seen in the practice of an organizer making a difference in history.

Again, one of the weaknesses of all organizers is a lack of introspection and taking the time to raise their own practice to the level of theory. At the Strategy Center, we take pride in our "theory driven practice and practice driven theory," but at times our work is undertheorized. We have a great work ethic that leads us to often skip the stage of the deepest sum-up of our work.

We carry out a fare strike, or a sit-in at the corner of Wilshire and Western, or a major legal challenge based on civil rights law, or the investment of thirty of our people at the U.S. Social Forum. We organize a sum-up with thirty-five or so people who gather for an evening for about three hours. Each person speaks for about five minutes; we write down some of the lessons and say we need an all-day retreat to sum up all the lessons and integrate them into a constantly expanding worldview based on practice. Then the next day we are pulled into the exigencies of mass practice, for there is another crisis, another opportunity, and the sum-up, in fact, is superficial and transitory. Sometimes, we do not take the time to stop the work to understand that summing up our own work, writing reports for ourselves and for the movement, is a critical part of our work. It is our work!

After more than four decades of "work," I have sat down for a few years to try to figure out what qualities among us lead to success and greatness, what do we strive for as people that is ethical, spiritual, strategic, tactical, and successful. Of course, with human beings, there are always inconsistencies, gaps, and flaws between our aspirations and our practice. Still, there is a deep connection between our psychological, personal, and political development, and in many ways, the sixteen qualities of the successful organizer are consistent with the qualities of a successful person and a successful life— one filled with meaning and a concern for others besides ourselves.

Joins an Organization
Based on Agreement with
Its Strategy and Tactics

An organizer is, by definition, a member of an organization. There is no theory of social change that involves individuals operating alone. The first step in the journey to change society is to join an organization. You join a group, and not just any group. People seeking their first organization often go through a trial-and-error period until they find the best match between their own politics and the politics of the group to which they want to make a long-term commitment. In most historical instances, there is a group already waiting for you that reflects your politics and is far more advanced along the road than you are.

The more developed, dedicated organizer joins a particular organization because she understands and agrees with its strategy, main tactics, and demands, and because she believes the organization can make history. Not only does she understand the politics of her group but she grasps that her group is situated within a larger movement—a broad alliance of groups, classes, races, nationalities, and organizations representing diverse interests and points of view. Under the best of conditions, this is more than a short-term or even long-term coalition. It is a strategic alliance, a united front of all who share common objectives.

Each organizer can only find hope, inspiration, and the dedication that is fundamental to success by joining the organization with which she agrees the most and, yes, the one she thinks is best at a particular time in history. A successful organizer studies the field and assesses the differences between groups. Then, she makes an informed decision and a commitment based on the deepest political unity. This foundation of unity is necessary because, when loyalty is tested, an organizer must stand on firm ground.

If you do not understand the politics of your own organization, understand its role in history, and believe that it is on the front lines of the battle, you will not stay long. You may participate in faction fights that undermine your organization. You may "shop" for other organizations or even believe you must create your own. These behaviors defeat the purpose of building an organization. For almost everyone, the best choice is to deliberate and then join an already existing organization, pay your dues, and dig in for the hard work of organizing.

Hard choices inside the Congress of Racial Equality

In the fall of 1964, I joined the Congress of Racial Equality (CORE) and was hired as a field secretary in the Northeast Regional Office in New York City. I believed that CORE, initiated in 1942, was the most militant and effective organization in the North. It also had a strong base in the South, working closely with the Student Nonviolent Coordinating Committee (SNCC). CORE initiated the Freedom Rides in 1961. The organization's national visibility expanded exponentially in 1964 when CORE field organizers Mickey Schwerner, Andrew Goodman, and James Chaney were martyred in Meridian, Mississippi. In New York, the Brooklyn and Bronx CORE chapters had invented the "stall-ins" that threatened to tie

up traffic on Long Island freeways if the city would not hire
Black and Puerto Rican construction workers for the 1964 U.S.
World's Fair.

When I was accepted as a CORE "field secretary" (CORE's
and SNCC's job title for a dedicated grassroots organizer), I
was thrilled and honored. In choosing CORE, I had sought out
a militant and grassroots organization.

I thought I had made all the choices that were necessary.
But in my first week of work, I was pulled aside for one-on-
one discussions by three individual Black leaders of the organization, impressive comrades who represented, as it turned
out, three different political tendencies of the organization:
the James Farmer group, the Bayard Rustin group, and the
Brooklyn/Bronx CORE group. Each one made the case for their
particular affiliation and tried to recruit me to their point of
view. This was very threatening to my twenty-one-year-old
soul. I thought I knew what I had joined, and now I was learning that CORE itself was split into three factions vying for the
strategic leadership of the organization. I had to rapidly rid
myself of illusions and become a quick study. Each faction
sought my allegiance and each was proposing radically different courses of action.

James Farmer, the director of CORE, was one of the leaders of the "Big Five" civil rights groups—SNCC, CORE, the
NAACP, Urban League, and Southern Christian Leadership
Council (SCLC). He had been on the Freedom Rides and, with
a booming voice, was the public face of CORE. He came out
of a multiracial, pacifist tradition and did not like the move
towards Black Power and street militancy that the younger
"Black militants" were proposing. He was close to the Democratic Party but did not want to be an appendage of it. While
he had opposed the stall-ins, given the internal politics of
CORE and the power of the militants, he was forced to hire
Herb Callender, the chair of Bronx CORE and one of the initia-
tors of the stall-ins, as a field secretary.

Bayard Rustin is appreciated today because he suffered
and stood up to homophobic treatment as a gay man in the

Black movement and helped to lead the March on Washington. Rustin wrote an influential article in *Commentary* magazine, "From Protest to Politics," in which he criticized the Black movement for having a narrow political vision and a fear of engaging the political system to win systemic reforms. He caricatured those who wanted to build an independent Left outside of the Democratic Party simply as "protestors." He equated "politics" with Democratic Party politics. His strategy, influential but not decisive at CORE, represented a different political perspective: to tie the Civil Rights Movement to the Democratic Party establishment.

The third tendency in CORE was the Black militant caucus led by Brooklyn CORE's Isaiah Brunson and Bronx CORE's Herb Callender. They too wanted to integrate protest and politics but felt the right strategy was to build an independent Black movement that could challenge and influence the Democrats and the Republicans—through the MFDP, the stall-ins, and opposition to the war in Vietnam. They supported CORE as a multiracial organization, but criticized CORE under Farmer's leadership for being too middle-class Black and too white at the chapter level. They wanted the urban and rural Black poor to have the decisive voice in the organization. In 1964, in my first months in the organization, I made an important choice. I had the most sympathy for the Black militant faction and the most fundamental disagreements with the Rustin faction. But I also made a tactical assessment of the situation that CORE, as such an important historical force, should stay intact rather than split into three separate organizations. I was a minor player in all these events but did express my views. I agreed with those who felt that, in order to keep the organization together, we needed a set of agreements on principled operational unity.

As usual, when I faced forks in the road, I tried to look for guidance in my organizing among the working-class Black and Puerto Rican people with whom I was working. At the time, I was the lead organizer for the Trailways bus boycott, in which the employment futures of hundreds of Black and Puerto Rican workers were at stake. In that context, we needed James Farmer as the national public figure, Herb Callender as our most militant spokesperson, and Joyce Ware, my strongest mentor, who sided with Rustin, as the most tactically sophisticated leader for the actual campaign. Because Joyce agreed that the challenge to Farmer should not be pursued, and because she had good relationships with the other two tendencies, she and I worked to win the Trailways fight and played a positive role by not contributing to any destructive "factionalizing" but rather to holding the organization together.

The organization held together for several more years. Still, the fight over Black Power versus joining the Johnson's administration's poverty program, and the fight over openly opposing the war in Vietnam, as Ruth Turner of Cleveland CORE advocated, versus not taking a position out of fear of isolating the organization, as James Farmer proposed, led to irreconcilable differences. Still, I had learned early in the game that making hard choices politically and organizationally was a requirement for a successful organizer. Sometimes you have to make choices to figure out how to hold an organization together; at other times the political differences are so profound that a split and separation is necessary. In each case, you join an organization based on your political assessment of who you believe is the leading force at the time. Your commitment to those choices becomes a critical component of your political identity and legacy. Throughout my work, I have tried to take responsibility for my own actions and to realize that when you join a successful organization, you have the best chance of collectively making history.

Builds a Base and
Never Walks Alone

There are many ways of assessing a successful organizer, but in the final analysis, it comes down to the quality and quantity of people that you have organized. For the organizer, having a base is the indisputable measurement of power and success in the field that is recognized by organizers of different politics and persuasions, elected officials, corporate executives, friends and foes. In that sense, success in organizing is empirically verifiable. It can be measured by the number of people you recruit, the months or years or decades they stay with an organization, and their capacity to lead. Numbers and members are measurements of the moral authority of your organization's program. They are measurements of the power of a movement and its likelihood to win. Your adversaries can count; they see votes, consumers, people with the power to curtail or undermine their objectives. The more numbers, the more members, the greater your bargaining power. Organizers who cannot recruit, who cannot bring new members to the organization, do not advance the organization's power to carry out its objectives. The organizer who shows up with a large group of members is understood to have a powerful base. She never walks alone, and she often wins the day.

Having a base is the difference between victory and defeat. It is a commonly agreed upon metric in the field of organizing that the organizers have to "make their numbers." There are groups with moderate or pragmatic worldviews that question the capacity of transformative organizers to build a base around their politics. Yet, they offer grudging admiration for your theory and your politics (and are sometimes actually won over to your point of view) if your group can bring an impressive number of members for an action at the corner of Western and Wilshire in Los Angeles or 125th Street and Malcolm X Boulevard/Lenox Avenue in Harlem. Making your numbers, delivering your base, does not lend itself to exaggeration. Whether you organize in a workplace; on a bus or street corner; in a church, school, or home, understand what your real capacity is and, with each action, work to meet and exceed those expectations, for your own credibility and that of the organization is at stake. Elected officials I have dealt with have told me in no uncertain terms that numbers count. Turning out your base is the key criterion by which an organization's influence is judged, by its friends and enemies. After all, it is the base that constitutes a social movement, and, with accurate analysis, strategy, and tactics, the base that fights to win social transformation.

The key to building a base is to be able to recruit enough organizers to impact the community so that each person's work generates a *multiplier effect*. In this multiplier-effect process, the success of each organizer becomes cumulative and then, when it reaches a critical mass, begins to be *qualitatively greater* as the community or workplace or bus becomes a stronghold for the group. In this process, the recruits eventually become organizers themselves who recruit new members, often friends, classmates, or members of their own family. Therefore, a central aspect of success is the organizer's (or organization's) ability to identify and recruit organic leadership, the persons among the oppressed who are already leaders in popular struggles and recognized in their workplace, church, or community as such. When you can recruit such advanced mass leaders to a more developed worldview and tactical plan, they, in turn, can bring other people into the organization—because they already have a base. An organizer who can activate this multiplier effect is a critical catalyst to social change.

Dolores Huerta: She never walks alone

A leader in the social justice movement since 1945, Dolores Huerta was been a prominent organizer in the United Farm Workers from 1960 to 2002. She always built a base and has talked, walked, and marched with dozens, hundreds, even tens of thousands of people.

Huerta began her lifetime of organizing when she was teenager in Stockton, California, during the last years of World War II. Her specialty was social events. A friend of the family offered his storefront for a teen center, and Huerta invited all her friends. They put in ping-pong tables and a jukebox and organized dance contests. "Then the police shut us down because we were a very integrated group and they didn't want these white girls hanging out with all these Mexicans and Pilipinos and Blacks," Huerta explains. "Even my first innocent organizing drew the police."

Huerta learned about serious organizing when Fred Ross Sr.—the legendary organizer of migrant workers camps during the Depression—came to Stockton in 1955 to organize a chapter of the Community Service Organization. "Two things about the CSO hooked me: They built a campaign around Ed Roybal, who was the first Latino elected to the L.A. City Council [and later California's first Latino member of Congress]. Then they got all these police sent to prison for beating up Latinos. I was ready to sign up because the police were always harassing us, starting with that little teen center that we had."

The CSO understood about building a base: going door-to-door to organize house meetings on voter registration, citizenship classes, electoral politics, and grassroots organizing to win vital social services—water, parks, recreation centers. The CSO recruited and trained organizers as base builders, including the young leaders Cesar Chavez and Dolores Huerta. Ross's house-meeting model was adopted by Huerta and Chavez. This is how Dolores explains how she built a base for the United Farm Workers (UFW) from 1959 to 1965 so that they could carry out and win their historic Delano, California, grape strike and boycott from 1965 to 1970.

It's a simple but difficult process. You begin with a lead, someone you think has the passion and will to invite six to eight people to a house meeting. Then you call them on the phone. Many farmworkers didn't have phones, so you went to visit them in their homes. Then you find someone to host the meeting at their home.

The six to eight number is critical. You don't want it any larger because it will inhibit people from participating; people don't speak up and they hold their thoughts back. In the intimate group, people are able to talk and you're able to get them to really engage the issues, and now you have a personal contact with them.

The UFW organizer gives a presentation at each meeting, but the important point is to get a strong host of the meeting. As they do all the work to prepare for the meeting—calling their friends, relatives, and coworkers to make sure they attend, thinking through the agenda with the organizer—they don't realize it, but they're actually organizing that meeting. They learn by doing. They become an organizer.

And then, out of each house meeting we get someone to host the next house meeting . . . and bring a new six to eight people. After we have involved two hundred people in house meetings, we call for a neigh-

borhood or citywide or ranchwide meeting. We elect
officers, and the group begins to carry out programs
to help the organizing work or help the strike or the
boycott. This is how we build our base. We are always
building our base. That is the key to organizing.

Chavez and Huerta used this method to organize up and
down the San Joaquin Valley. Huerta took San Joaquin, Stan-
islaus, and Merced counties, and Chavez took Kern, Tulare,
Fresno, and Kings. They organized dozens of house meetings
in each county and then brought their 150 to 200 people together at a larger gathering. That created the base for the first
convention, on September 30, 1962, where they made the historic decision to form the National Farm Workers Association,
an alliance of Pilipino and Mexican workers—a predecessor of
the United Farm Workers Union. Philip Veracruz, a leader
of the Pilipino workers, was another great farmworker pio-
neer and helped the unity of Pilipino and Mexican workers.

In 1965, when they began the first grape strike and boycott, they felt they had built a solid base because they had
organized the workers for years before the strike to understand what they would be facing. They generated the multiplier effect, organizing hundreds of worker leaders who
in turn reached tens of thousands of farmworkers to build
a movement that forced the powerful Gallo Winery, Schen-
ley Liquors, and other grape-growing corporations to sign a
union contract with the UFW.

Dolores recounts, "Once Cesar told me, 'We have to have
a very long perspective because we may not see a farmworkers union in our lifetime—the growers are too powerful, too
rich, and too racist.' But we surprised ourselves and did see it
in our lifetime."

One reason for their success was the direct and honest
conversations organizers pursued with the workers. Dolores remembers, "We would say, 'First of all, nobody is going
to change your conditions unless you do it. You have to do it
yourselves. The next thing is that you have power. You may

not have money. You may not speak English. You may not be a citizen. But you have power and the power is in your person, but it's not going to work unless you get together with other people to make it happen.'"

I asked Dolores Huerta what she considers the greatest achievements of her long and continuing life of service and struggle. The first, she said, was the building of the UFW, which still exists today, forty years later, as an institution that has become permanent and has more than 20,000 workers under union contract. The second was that she is a leader in the Feminization of Power campaign to encourage more women to run for public office. Through her work with the Feminist Majority and other women's organizations, this campaign was able to elect U.S. senator Barbara Boxer, Los Angeles County Supervisor Gloria Molina, and California State Assembly members Martha Escutia, Hilda Solis, Gloria Romero, and (now Congresswoman) Karen Bass.

Her third-greatest achievement, Dolores said, is building the Dolores Huerta Foundation, where she is training a new generation of organizers to fight for women's rights, abortion rights, and immigration and labor rights. "We need to recreate a single movement," she concluded, "because with everyone fighting for gay rights, workers rights, civil rights— unless we are working for everyone's rights at the same time around a common political program, we will be isolated and ineffective."

On her eightieth birthday, celebrated at the Greek Theater in Los Angeles in 2010, nearly six thousand people filled every seat to honor her—including actors Martin Sheen, Alfre Woodard, Benjamin Bratt; elected officials Congressman Raul Grijalva, Secretary of Labor Hilda Solis (mentioned earlier as an assemblywoman), Los Angeles mayor Antonio Villaraigosa; and musicians Carlos Santana and Pete Escovedo. That is a reflection of having a base you can deliver—and even better, one that wants to deliver for you as well.

Sings with the Choir
but Finds Her Own Voice

The successful organizer begins by learning collective discipline, the strategic direction of the group, and the organizational culture in which they are situated. Without a clear plan and everyone's allegiance to it, an organization can't move forward. But there must be room for originality and, yes, individuality—otherwise a rigid organizational culture can kill all creativity and excellence and prevent success. A successful organizer must be adept at negotiating this balance and projecting her own voice while singing with the choir.

When I teach the Organizer's Exchange at the Strategy Center, I often use the example of Art Blakey and the Jazz Messengers to illustrate the concept of "sings with the choir and finds her own voice." The Jazz Messengers were one of the most impressive and formative "straight-ahead" jazz ensembles of the 1960s, '70s, and '80s. Their signature song was "Moanin'." The number begins with a haunting, soulful refrain that all five members of the quintet play in unison. Then, one by one, beginning with Lee Morgan on trumpet, followed by tenor sax man Benny Golson, and ending with the pianist (and the song's composer) Bobby Timmons, they deliver brilliantly improvised solos and riffs off the main theme. Each solo is punctuated with drum rolls by Art Blakey, the percussionist and leader of the group. The entire melody is backed up by the rhythmic and harmonic anchor of bassist Jymie Merritt. At the end of the song, Blakey brings the group together with another drum roll, and they return to the main theme, the reprise, where they end in powerful, soulful harmony. They make a great choir, but each one is also a soloist, finding his own voice.

At the height of the antiwar and Civil Rights movements in the 1960s, the mass rally was an important tactic to show the government we had a strong base and to build the solidarity of our troops. We would end every march with speakers who were great orators and performers, each one with such a distinctive style and a very specific message. Howard Zinn confronted the establishment and the war machine with sarcasm, ridicule, and a sense of moral outrage. Fannie Lou Hamer, born a sharecropper in Rueville, Mississippi, warned people that Vietnam was the Democrats' war and, speaking for the entire Black working class, announced, "I am sick and tired of being sick and tired." Abbie Hoffman told young people to burn their money, steal his book, and break with the rampant materialism of capitalism. Martin Luther King Jr. used his majestic, booming voice and the power of the social gospel to demand an end to racism, poverty, and militarism. Malcolm X, a biting orator with a ferocious sense of humor, ridiculed the white power structure for enslaving Black people mentally and physically. He called for Black people to seek their liberation, influenced by Jean Paul Sartre, by "any means necessary." Ericka Huggins had a personal, deeply authentic style that called for support of the Black Panther Party's Ten-Point Program, their Breakfast for Children Program, their call to free Huey Newton and all political prisoners, and the role of Black women on the front lines of the revolution. They disagreed over some tactics and approaches, but they all called for complete U.S. withdrawal from Vietnam and the strongest civil rights protections, affirmative action, voting rights, and a new social welfare state that addressed structural poverty and racism. What a choir they made.

At the end of these performance pieces, the marchers would be deeply moved, with a new set of ideas to drive their daily work as they went back to their communities. It was the passion and originality of each speaker that gave us hope, for this was a movement with many voices, many angles on the same problem, in which the differentiation of style with the similarity of content was one of its great achievements. This choir was replicated in every community with a new set of speakers, each with their own voices, creativity, and oratorical power. This choir with many voices was instrumental in building a mass movement of tens of millions, so powerful and visible that a beleaguered president Richard Nixon was forced to describe right-wing, prowar people as a "silent majority."

In 2001 in Durban, South Africa, and in 2002 in Johannesburg, I marched with the Congress of South African Trade Unions (COSATU) in protests against the neoliberal policies that were keeping power in the same white, rich, corporate hands. The slogans were moving: "We did not fight against apartheid to deliver the country to the highest bidder" and "Socialism, build it now." The march captains showed us many dance steps and got great pleasure in teaching their international comrades their first Zulu chants. We marched for four hours. Even among the most talented Black masses, there were the stars who stood out—great dancers, great chanters, great drummers, great agitators who led the charge along the march route. The South African tradition of the toi toi, the combination of marches, dancing, chanting, singing, and bringing a unified chorus against an adversary, is one of the highest forms of mass protest and involves hundreds of thousands of people singing with the choir and finding their own voices.

One reflection of the movement-building power of consciously training leadership that can speak for the movement and speak for themselves is when the Bus Riders Union organized its campaign against "The MTA's Racist Fare Hike" in 2006. The campaign was covered on seven different television stations in English, Spanish, and Korean, and the BRU had seven different spokespeople. Each person was carefully chosen and carefully trained, for the stakes of "staying on message" were high; and each person sparkled under questioning from reporters. Shepherd Petit, Grandma Hee Pok Kim, Carla Gonzalez, Esperanza Martinez, Francisca Porchas, Barbara Lott-Holland, and Sunyoung Yang demonstrated to those who were viewing the programs that the organization had a strong and diverse group of leaders and made them feel that they would be welcomed and appreciated if they joined.

There are times when an entire organization knows it is on a roll, is in gear, is hitting its stride, is playing a great song in history. Great organizing has its transcendent moments when the entire organization is in harmony. And yet, the individual solos take the group higher as key leaders and members get power and confidence from each other's artistry. The group agrees on the theme, on the main melody, on the foundation from which all its members will improvise. Then, after the most creative and interpretive solos, they come back together, to sing the same song with one voice, so the system can feel the power of their unified force.

A Good Listener:
Keeps an Ear to the Ground

One of the greatest qualities of the successful organizer is the ability to listen: listen to your base, listen to peers, listen to criticism. Listening is a centerpiece of any successful social practice and of any good relationship based on equality among people. It is the building block of a dialectical, transformative theory of organizing—for an organizer can only understand the validity and limits of his theory by listening to and learning from the people he is organizing. Listening allows the organizer to develop a clear picture of the lived realities and the ideas of the working class. This creates a process by which to plan strategy and tactics: a process for understanding the operations of the system; the concrete conditions of the working class at any given time, place, and conditions; the contradictions that define the challenge; and the actual consciousness, willingness, and capacity of the oppressed to fight. Of course, listening is essential in building any successful relationship. In the organizing process, it is critical to recruiting people into an organization and, further, retaining them.

While I've been a good listener in much of my own practice, at times I have not listened well and at great cost.

Listening to criticism from comrades and engaging in self-reflection have offered me the road to redemption and re-unified action.

The art of listening: CORE and the Trailways bus boycott

As a field secretary with CORE, I worked with an already organized group of Black and Puerto Rican porters at the Trailways Bus Company who were demanding to be hired as bus drivers, ticket agents, and information clerks, jobs then held only by whites.

It began in the fall of 1964, when I received a phone call from Eddie Barnes, an angry Black porter at Trailways. He told me a story about how he had been denied access to a better-paying and more skilled position at the bus company. But by the time he'd called me that day, I had already answered more than twenty phone calls. Most of them were heartbreaking individual stories—a Black man had been cheated by a car salesman, a tenant by her landlord, a family by a local merchant—which I listened to with great empathy but still had to answer, "I'm really sorry. CORE doesn't handle individual discrimination cases." In those cases, I would refer the person to a city or state civil rights commission (which had only recently been brought into being by the Civil Rights Movement) or to an attorney who handled individual civil rights violations, and I urged them to get involved in their local CORE chapter.

But Eddie Barnes was insistent this was not an individual case; there were a group of workers at Trailways who wanted to fight a group discrimination case and were looking to CORE for direct action. They were Black and Puerto Rican porters, the men who carried the passengers' bags. They had been denied promotions to better-paying jobs that were filled by white workers: information clerks, ticket agents, and bus drivers. Barnes would not take no for an answer. He explained that it would be a great collaboration between the Trailways workers and CORE. I remember being so relieved that my exhaustion from listening to so many individual complaints had not led me to dismiss what would turn out to be such a historic civil rights struggle. I set up a meeting the next day with a group of ten Trailways workers.

I listened to the workers' stories in great detail, trying to assess if they had a strong factual case, one that we could win in the court of public opinion, in the courts, or in front of government agencies. "Big Sam" and Noel Quiñones stood out, along with Eddie, as great public representatives. I was convinced that the workers' claims were just and true and that they had the fighting capacity to really make this a struggle, not simply a group grievance. We began studying civil rights laws, interstate commerce clauses, and Trailways' history of hiring as well as its corporate structure. As tacticians, we were looking for weak spots in the enemy's armor and places against which CORE could apply pressure.

I was selected by both CORE and the Trailways workers as the lead organizer of the campaign. We began the campaign with a civil rights march at the Port Authority bus terminal, near Times Square on Eighth Avenue in Manhattan. The campaign got excellent media coverage, including front-page stories in the *New York Times*, which gave momentum and credibility to our movement. In the early stages of the campaign, I was its main spokesperson. Our main demand was that Trailways hire a significant number of Black and Puerto Rican workers in key positions immediately. Our key tactic was to ask Black bus riders in particular and others in general, to boycott Trailways until our demands were won. When I spoke to the press or appeared on radio or TV, I implored the readers, listeners, and viewers to boycott Trailways.

My immediate supervisor and first mentor at CORE, Joyce Ware, made a major intervention in the campaign. She explained that while she was glad that I had listened to the workers in planning the campaign and thought my organizing work with the workers showed real dedication, my role as a spokesperson was ineffective. I had a gift for making the case briefly and clearly on TV and made Trailways nervous because I was winning the argument in front of white liberal audiences and government agencies. But, Joyce explained that I had not studied the situation carefully and that my main arguments were not based on an understanding of the actual conditions of Black people's lives. She said that my too-frequent TV appearances reflected arrogance.

What I learned by listening to Joyce's criticism was a painful truth—I hadn't been listening enough. I had listened well to the workers but not enough to the community we were trying to enlist. The corrective was to listen to the tough-love advice of my supervisor. My exhortations to the Black community to support the boycott were ineffective, because no one from Harlem would look at me as a white person and think for a moment that I was making the same sacrifice that I was asking them to make.

The cost for a Black Harlem resident to boycott Trailways might involve not traveling back to the Black Belt South, their historic homeland where so many northern Blacks still had many family members, until the campaign was over. Effective agitation would have to acknowledge that painful choice and address it squarely. We would be asking people to make this sacrifice for the cause, to break the back of Trailways so that Blacks could smash employment racism in transportation. The long-term vision was that Black people in the North could then go back to the South with a Black woman or man driving the bus.

Joyce proposed that I remain as the lead organizer of the campaign but that Herb Callender, a well-known and respected Black leader from Bronx CORE, should become the primary public spokesperson. I asked myself why I hadn't understood that to be the right decision without having to be told. I had to learn to really put the interests of the Black masses at the heart of my work. Once Joyce explained it, the decision was obvious, and the move to replace me with Herb was in the best interests of our goal to force Trailways to hire and promote large numbers of Black and Puerto Rican workers. I was fully on board.

We spent a year breaking down Trailways' doors. In New York, Philadelphia, Baltimore, and Washington, D.C., we held up the entire terminal by asking directions for trips with twenty destinations and buying tickets with pennies. In a year of nonstop organizing, I commuted up and down the East Coast, working with CORE chapters.

At the end of that year, I got a call from Eddie Barnes, who the day before was still carrying folks' bags. He said, "Come to the Port Authority, look around and you'll see me." When I got there, Eddie was standing behind the information counter, working with customers who wanted to go wherever the bus would take them. On his break, Eddie and I walked around the Port Authority. "Eric, look what we've done," he said. "There are Black and Brown faces all over the place, in every store, food stand. Hundreds of new jobs here, hundreds more in every city we covered."

Listening to the working class: Lian teaches how to listen

One of the decisive experiences in my life was what we now call "The Gene and Rita Story," in which my partner, Lian, taught me about listening. She explained, in theory and practice, the danger of "running through stop signs," that is, failing to pause and really understand what's being communicated to you.

In 1976, Lian and I were workers at the Ford Milpitas Assembly Plant outside of San Jose, following that tactical plan of working in both the auto industry and the United Auto Workers (UAW). One of our objectives—and an idea floated by many progressive shop-floor workers as well—was to build a "rank and file caucus" against both the company and the conservative forces in the union. The goal was to consolidate a group of the most militant and class-conscious workers of Local 560 at the Ford plant, as well as to help build a national militant-workers tendency in the UAW.

Gene and Rita, another married couple, also both worked at the plant. Rita was relatively new, having gotten into Ford about the same time as Lian. They were among the first women ever hired at Ford as part of the company's efforts to comply with federal civil rights statutes mandating the hiring of more women. Once in, Lian was instrumental in getting me hired. Gene was a Ford veteran; he had more than twenty years at the plant and was a very influential voice among the workers. Gene and Rita were a white Southern couple who were militantly antiracist and our greatest hope for solid working-class white members. They befriended us as a couple, and trusted us in the fight for a better union and the fight against racism. They valued our willingness to stand up to the company supervisors on the shop floor, who were always pushing the workers to work faster and faster. Gene and Rita's participation in the caucus was essential because they were what we called "the advanced workers," the progressive leaders of the class who could bring many other workers with them.

One evening, Lian and I went over to their house for dinner. Gene and Rita had been great with us when we bought our modest home in the Milpitas neighborhood adjacent to the Ford plant. As Gene told us, "Well, the good thing about buying a house is you'll never have a problem about figuring out something to do every day." We went to dinner with the intent to have fun, and with the tactical objective of getting Gene and Rita to agree to the caucus idea.

After dinner we went into the living room and I made a presentation to them proposing that they join us in organizing a new rank-and-file caucus in the union local. There was a silence. Then Gene and Rita started talking about refinishing the wood on their beautiful staircase. I waited, impatiently and already somewhat angrily, for some small talk to pass and again repeated the same appeal, seeking new angles to make the case, if perhaps more aggressively. They responded by talking about the best ideas about how to repave the driveway. Each time, Lian followed their lead and enthusiastically talked about stairways and driveways.

When we left, I felt the evening had been a total failure, and I was angry at the situation and at Lian. "Did you not see where I was going?" I argued. "I thought we had both agreed to ask them to join the caucus. You left me hanging out there to dry."

Lian had some anger of her own: "Eric, did you not listen? Do you think they didn't hear you? Obviously they didn't want to form a caucus, or at least not now. Maybe they are afraid of too much association with a left initiative. I don't know. But do you think they were talking about their house by accident? They were saying no loud and clear, but you refused to listen. Wouldn't it be better to let it pass and re-approach them at work in a way to ask questions instead of giving answers, to really listen to their thinking and try to understand if we can address their concerns?"

I replayed the situation through Lian's eyes and saw myself in a very unattractive light—arrogant and even pig-headed. It was one of those "teachable moments" where I had to replay the entire evening over and over so the lesson would burn itself into my brain. I have always been a forceful and persuasive person but also thought of myself as a good lis-tener as well. I understood the difference between cogently presenting an idea versus trying to "sell" it. I knew how to take time to listen to the response. Then, based on the in-formation you received, either realize the initial proposal wasn't that well thought out or effective, or, if you still feel convinced the idea is helpful, enter into a process of nego-tiation to address the person's concerns: what would make it worthwhile to join the organization, and what adjustments in the caucus idea would encourage her to join it? But, in this case, it was obvious that, under that time, place, and condi-tions, Gene and Rita did not want to have that conversation. I wasn't listening; Lian was. Again, I learned by listening to criticism.

A few months later, through self-criticism and self-correction, Lian and I continued to talk to Gene and Rita about joining. They had more to lose than many of us and had a lot of hard questions to be answered before they wanted to be part of a caucus. One thing that reassured them was that the vast majority of workers in the caucus were sophisticated in carrying out their organizing work in the plant in a way that neutralized company attacks on union militants and had the know-how to navigate the complex politics of our local union. Finally, they joined, and provided leadership and great moral authority for the caucus among the workers. They agreed with our tactic to run a slate of delegates for union office who would oppose the forced overtime, the violations of health and safety standards, and the grueling speed-ups. Eight of us ran for office, including William and Mercedes, another couple we were close to, and Lian and me. With twenty members of the caucus, we connected with every worker in the plant, and we were getting a lot of support when we campaigned on the shop floor.

On election day, none of us got elected, though we received more than 20 percent of the vote. This was very impressive for a new caucus in a plant dominated by old-line politicians. We had run a fine campaign and had raised our visibility and prestige in the local. We met many workers who voted for us against the established union leadership and many others who had at least considered it. That day, as we were still outside the union hall handing out leaflets to the last straggling voters, Gene and Rita drove out of the union parking lot after having voted. They yelled out their windows, with great pride in their voices, "Well, as we tell all our friends, we ended up voting for you damn radicals, and we're glad we did!"

One of my strengths as a lead organizer is to bring great enthusiasm and new ideas to the movement. Since that is my role, being a good listener, a great listener, is critical. That is how we learn, how we build trust with coworkers and comrades. Others will listen to us when they know we are carefully listening to them. That's why it's essential to be part of an organization, so that, as in this case, I could have my comrade Lian double-check my work and argue for her own tactical plan, which she thought was better. As with all successful qualities, you don't exhibit them all of the time. When done correctly, however, the practice of self-criticism, self-reflection, and self-correction can turn a defeat into a victory.

A Good Investigator:
Seeks Truth from Facts

A good organizer, especially the great tacticians and strategists, must have the capacity to make detailed investigations of concrete conditions; to base his theory of social change on the actual conditions of working-class life, and to envision the greatest historical possibilities in each situation. A good investigator is a good listener, and the great organizers raise listening to a higher level of theory, integrating insights gleaned from the people into a detailed battle plan.

One of the most compelling models of the organizer as investigator is Wyndham Mortimer. Mortimer was the lead organizer of the fledgling United Auto Workers, and was part of the great wave of industrial unionism initiated by the Congress of Industrial Organizations (CIO). While Bob Travis was the master of the moment, Mortimer was the group builder, the foundation builder, the organizer to sometimes construct movements with his own bare hands. They already had a great tactical plan: to take over the two GM plants that made the dies for all GM plants, the Cleveland plant and Fisher Body #1 in Flint, Michigan. Mortimer was sent into Flint to do the advance scouting and investigation necessary to come up with a more specific tactical plan. Mortimer observed, "I began by making a survey of the problem facing me. I spent a week asking questions and gathering information." Mortimer knew that GM and Ford were filled with company spies. As part of his investigation, he tried to uncover the network of snitches and informants that he would have to outmaneuver in order to reach the class-conscious workers.

Mortimer reached out to a woman janitor who worked in the offices of Chevrolet management in Flint. He asked her if she would give him the papers from the wastebasket that the company had her burn every day.

> Looking over the material I was amazed. Numerous slips of paper would read something like this, "Today at lunch, badge number so and so hid a copy of the union newspaper in his lunch box." Signed G8 or whatever his symbol was. Many auto workers lost their jobs without knowing why. The answers were to be found in those reports [from company spies].

Armed with the new fruits of his investigation, Mortimer moved on with more confidence, and caution, to reach out to the workers. Through his investigation, he discovered, not to his great surprise, that many of the white workers who supported the union were anti-Black. Yet, through his own values and his political training he understood that the union drive would fail unless the UAW welcomed and protected the rights of Black workers.

Mortimer met with a leading Black worker, "Old Jim," who in turn directed him to his son-in-law, Henry Clark. Buick employed about four thousand Black people, but they faced so much racism from both the company and the white workers that they had questions as to whether they would join a union at all. Through dogged organizing, he was able to set up a clandestine meeting with a group of Black workers in a small church late at night. He acknowledged the racism of many of the white workers and pledged that the new UAW would have a strong antiracist posture and would protect Black workers from company discrimination. Any organizer knows that is virtually unheard of to have a meeting of eighteen workers and to have all eighteen join the union and pay initiation fees on the spot, especially in the middle of the night. But those were the conditions that led to the successful growth of the UAW and the organizing victories against General Motors.

From 1936 to 1937, the UAW carried out the great Flint sit-down strike. Mortimer was one of the leaders of that historic breakthrough in labor history, when unarmed but militant workers occupied GM's factories and won union recognition. His good investigation set the conditions for that victory.

Bus Riders Union: The planning committee plans

When in 1996 the Los Angeles County Metropolitan Transportation Authority (MTA) refused to implement its agreements to reduce overcrowding, the Bus Riders Union planning committee envisioned a No Seat, No Fare campaign. Were bus riders angry about the overcrowded conditions on the buses? Were they willing to take action to remedy the problem by refusing to pay their bus fare if they didn't have a seat? We needed to verify the factual basis upon which to carry out the campaign or our campaign would fail. So, the planning committee sent fifteen organizers into the field to have lengthy discussions with bus riders.

The feedback was reported in a complex and informed manner. Of the approximately 850 people we spoke with, a hundred said they would refuse to pay the fare to stop the overcrowding. Two hundred said they thought the conditions on the bus were unbearable, but about half said it was immoral not to pay the fare even if they had to stand. Another hundred were ambivalent but leaning towards refusing to pay. Another hundred did not focus on the campaign but on the Bus Riders Union itself; they did not know enough about the BRU and had questions about whether they could trust our leadership. Another hundred said they supported the moral issues of the strike but were undocumented and feared retaliation and deportation. Another fifty were young people with "strikes," prior offenses due to the California's "Three-Strikes Law," and were afraid of being arrested and sent back to prison for parole violation. And the remaining few hundred had no opinion.

From those complex assessments, the good investigator begins to get the lay of the land, especially concerning "the contradictions among the people." The transformative organizer can come back to the people, address their questions, and try to change the empirical conditions on the ground. In the case of the No Seat, No Fare campaign, our investigation led us to make several tactical changes.

First, we decided to announce the campaign publicly ninety days before we planned to initiate it. That was risky, because we tipped off the MTA and put our reputation on the line. If we had continued to try to pick up support quietly, we could have decided not to carry out the plan if the response wasn't strong enough. But we made the assessment from our first round of investigation that there was great outrage about the actual conditions on the bus. We could not translate that anger into action without giving people enough time to realize this thing was really going to happen. This put even greater pressure on our organizers to build up support—which traditionally has led to better results. We could not really get people to take action until we announced the kick-off date. Now they understood the No Seat, No Fare campaign was really going to happen. Now we would find out who was really on board. Through hundreds of one-on-one conversations with riders and bus drivers, dozens of times we spoke to the whole group of passengers in three languages, tens of thousands of flyers distributed, and strong media coverage, we could see the campaign was hitting its stride. We made the case that refusing to pay was a moral choice consistent with the traditions of civil disobedience against a government agency that was taking their tax money and bus fare and not providing equality of service based on race. We told the riders, "Don't pay for transit racism."

On August 11, 1998, we held a well-attended press conference and initiated the No Seat No Fare campaign. The positive responses were far greater than we had anticipated: for once, a critical mass of bus riders refused to pay. It generated a multiplier effect where others got more courage and tapped into more anger. This was also encouraged by the bus drivers with whom we had worked persistently for months. They didn't like the overcrowded buses either; they disliked always having to tell people to move back, having arguments with riders. They also realized that our key demand was for the MTA to buy a lot more buses, which would provide more jobs for drivers, mechanics, and maintenance people.

In the end, an estimated ten thousand bus riders participated in the No Seat, No Fare campaign. The struggle on the buses with riders, drivers, and sometimes the MTA police was intense. Through court challenges, great media coverage, a sympathetic public, and a decent man at the helm of the MTA in CEO Julian Burke, the pressure worked. The MTA (with a court order behind the BRU) began to buy the first several hundred of what turned out to be 2,500 new compressed natural gas buses. The victories in the campaign began with a two-month intensive investigation process and based on that investigation we found the tools to win.

Tribune of the People:
Fights for All the Oppressed

A tribune of the people is a leader who fights against self-interested or even group-interested organizing among her own people and replaces it with a transformative view of social change. Examples of tribunes of the people include a Latina community organizer who fights for affirmative action for Blacks instead of insisting that "only Latinos are hard working and deserve the jobs," a white radical feminist who fights for the interests of Third World women inside and outside the United States, a Black worker who supports unconditional amnesty for Latino immigrants and gets his union to support the legal rights of gays to marry.

Many community organizers during the 1960s and even today have seen that militant community residents who are upset at specific manifestations of economic exploitation and racial discrimination will suddenly come out with the most strong antigay sentiments or antiwomen attitudes or virulently prowar opinions. A tribune of the people is an educator who raises the political consciousness of the people with whom she is working to an international level. In particular, she generates antiwar sentiments among the oppressed so they do not give their lives and those of their children to U.S. wars that are against their class, race, and gender interests.

In that spirit, during the 1930s, thousands of progressive and revolutionary-minded people left the United States to become soldiers in the Spanish Civil War. They fought to defend a democratically elected prosocialist government from being overthrown by Francisco Franco's fascist movement. They formed the Abraham Lincoln Brigade, which was also the first American military unit to be commanded by a Black officer, Oliver Law. These Americans joined leftists all over the world, who organized international brigades to support the Spanish government—"the loyalists." Sadly, the U.S. government under Franklin Roosevelt, ostensibly neutral or antifascist, prevented U.S. citizens from getting passports to Spain to fight with the loyalists. So, American citizens had to get passports to nearby countries and then find their way to Spain—already taking on their own government just to have the chance to fight in solidarity. All of these people went to a foreign land to risk their lives in the battle against fascism, a cause that was not naturally "their own." From 1936 to 1939, it is estimated that three thousand people from the United States joined the brigade, almost half of whom lost their lives in combat. It is in the actions of those men and women that we understand what it means to be a tribune of the people.

Audre Lorde: A tribune of the people

Audre Lorde was a warrior poet and revolutionary Black lesbian who was a true tribune of the people. She was always an intellectual fighter, often the lone wolf on any faculty panel, with the capacity to expose and challenge dominant categories of class, race, and gender studies. Working among white feminists in struggle against patriarchy, especially in the university, she challenged their racism. Rooted in the Black community, she also fought to bring down the walls of patriarchy, misogyny, and homophobia in Black society.

Through her roots in the Black Caribbean, she connected her work to Grenada, Cuba, and other sites of struggles for self-determination.

One of her most famous essays, a great example of agitational prose, was "The Master's Tools Will Never Dismantle the Master's House," written in 1979. She argued that the white women's movement, feeling threatened by rather than welcoming the contributions of Black, poor, lesbian, and older women, was isolating itself from its own strength. Lorde observed:

> If white women's American feminist theory need not deal with the differences between us, and the resulting difference in our oppressions, then how do you deal with the fact that the women who clean your houses and tend to your children while you attend conferences on feminist theory are, for the most part, poor women and women of Color? What is the theory behind racist feminism?

She raised this challenge to generate a more difficult and more honest process for building deeper unity. She argued that racism, sexism, and homophobia were inextricably intertwined in the system of imperialism and only a women's movement that addresses all of those oppressions in the context of a struggle against the system would have a chance at collective liberation.

In her own life, she used "coming out" as a political concept of transparency and self-love, which did not make it any less difficult in academic settings. In her poem "Blackstudies," she describes how she told her students she had "loved other tall young women deep into their colour" and, with apprehension, wanted them to understand her for who she really was. In the midst of this daring intellectual and cultural work Audre Lorde was also working with college faculty and artists who gave attention to organized political activism. She was the ultimate affiliated intellectual whose set of "causes" ran the full spectrum of left opposition to the system itself.

In her role as a faculty member, in 1969, she was part of a major struggle at the City University of New York for open admissions, demanding that Black and Latino students, regardless of income and performance on standardized testing, could attend college without discriminatory entrance exams. The students took over the university, and many classes moved to I.S. 201, a famous alternative Black high school run by local parents. Lorde moved her classes to the off-campus school, now called "Harlem University."

She was already a radical activist and a movement person. Even as she struggled to build the women's movement from within, Lorde also saw herself as part of the Black Liberation Movement. She did not support women's or lesbian separatism on the one hand or Black cultural nationalism on the other. She wanted Black women, independently organized, to reach out to Black men from a position of power and a common struggle. In her essay "Learning from the Sixties," she railed against the deep tensions inside the Black community and the Black movement's failure to accept full women's liberation and lesbians as part of the Black united front. She commented, "Hopefully, we can learn from the sixties that we cannot afford to do our enemies' work by destroying each other." And she quoted Malcolm X, "We are not responsible for our oppression, but we must be responsible for our own liberation."

Together with Barbara Smith, Demita Frazier, and Beverly Smith, Lorde helped form the Combahee River Collective in 1974. They defended Kenneth Edelin, a Black doctor in a Boston hospital arrested for manslaughter after he performed an abortion. And they supported the Third World Workers Coalition in demanding that Black workers, mainly men, be hired in Boston's notoriously racist construction unions to build a new high school.

When twelve Black women were murdered in the Boston area, they stood up as champions of the people. They struggled with the police over their racism in giving such a big case so little attention and placing such low value on Black women's lives. At the same time, they also challenged Black men who wanted to address the murders solely as cases of racist suppression, as if gender and the tendencies of misogyny and chauvinism in the community toward women had nothing to do with it. They put out a pamphlet, "Six Black Women: Why Did They Die?," which talked about the role of sexual violence against women. They offered self-defense strategies and referrals to Boston-based groups dealing with violence against women. In the end, many people in the Black community, the women's movement, and the Left, who were at first threatened by this militant group of Black feminists and lesbians, came to see that these very women were among the best fighters for the cause.

Several years later, Lorde would connect this dream to the most structural demands against racism, poverty, and war as a speaker at the 1983 "We Still Have a Dream" march on Washington, twenty years after Martin Luther King Jr.'s "I Have a Dream" speech. Lorde called for full employment, affirmative action, and an end to the system of patriarchy. Audre Lorde began her search for identity and justice as a Black lesbian. She never deviated from the core but expanded her vision to fight for multiple noble causes and was a true tribune of the people.

Generosity of Spirit:
Takes Good Care of Others

The transformative organizer is a fighter, courageous and effective in battle, and resolute in struggling to transform the consciousness of the community. But the transformative organizer must also be deeply generous, "guided by a great feeling of love," as Che Guevara once said.

When we hold ourselves open to listening and to giving, even when we must stretch ourselves to do so, generosity of spirit opens us to seeing the beauty of the people with whom we work, without romanticizing or idealizing them. It is fundamental to the complex mix of qualities of the successful organizer. At a time when our campaigns often seem to run steeply uphill and structural change seems far in the distance, we derive great solace and great energy from our struggle to create organizations and movements based on generosity of spirit.

One of the most useful places to look for and measure generosity of spirit is in the established regular meetings of an organization. Transformative organizers can find so many rituals and roles, both big and small, in which to develop, measure, and cultivate their own generosity of spirit—for like every other quality, there is a great deal of self-improvement possible.

The Bus Riders Union's monthly membership meeting, going on twenty years straight, is one of the richest examples to have shaped my own consciousness.

I'm reminded of Rosalio Mendiola, a Mexicano room-service waiter who has worked for thirty years at the Beverly Wilshire Hotel, one of the better working-class jobs in the city. Once a month, he is also the breakfast chef-in-residence for the Bus Riders Union (BRU).

Rosalio's days off are Fridays and Saturdays. On the third Friday of the month, Rosalio, accompanied by an organizer-in-training, uses his day off to do a massive food shop for the BRU to feed the one hundred members who will come to the general membership meeting. On Saturday, Rosalio arrives early to set up and cook for the forthcoming 10:00 a.m. crowd. The large room we rent at the Immanuel Presbyterian Church has a wonderful kitchen with refrigerator, stove, and grill, and a large counter where the food can be presented. Rosalio and Joe Ito, his assistant, put out a spread of bagels, cream cheese, Mexican *pan dulce*, croissants, fruit, yogurt, and, my favorite, his right-off-the-grill quesadillas that he custom makes for each member, with two homemade salsas to choose from. Our organization has a great culture of culinary solidarity, so I know that the sumptuous free breakfast is one reason that many members come to the meeting every month. It also sets a wonderful tone and mood for the meeting.

Rosalio was never assigned the job of providing the breakfast. It was his idea from the beginning, a great use of the members' dues money, and over the years it has become an essential part of the culture and ritual of the BRU monthly meeting. Rosalio's generosity is not simply an individual character trait. It reflects the collectivity and culture of an organization—a beautiful cross-section of working-class humanity. At every meeting, BRU members discuss conditions on the bus, conditions in the city, and conditions in the world—with great gusto, in Korean, Spanish, and English. As low-income, working-class people, the BRU's members are under a great deal of stress and strain every day. The BRU meetings bring together Koreans, Blacks, Latinos, and whites whose communities are mostly separate from each other. You might expect people to be testy, impatient, or too worn down to be very generous with each other. And yet it is so striking the way members do not require everyone to be on their best behavior and appreciate that everyone has overcome difficult conditions just to get to the meeting.

Generosity of spirit is what guides our best instincts in relating to our comrades and our people. Even as we push each other and our members to win, we must also create what organizer Tammy Bang Luu calls a "zone of tolerance" in which we accept each others' weaknesses and errors, and give each other room to breathe and to evolve into the best versions of ourselves. Sometimes members speak for too long; other times they miss the point of the agenda by wanting to tell the individual horror stories of their daily commute on the Metropolitan Transportation Authority bus system. In those cases, members are gently asked to stay on time and on point, but with considerable latitude, because they need to vent and where else would other people listen? Other times, members, especially Spanish and Korean monolingual women, do not speak at all. In this case they need encouragement from the chair and the offer of preparation for the next meeting, because we have found time and time again that some of the best ideas come from people who do not think their ideas are important or would be welcomed. The "zone of tolerance" is good psychology, group dynamics, and good politics.

The Newark Community Union Project: Terry Jefferson and her forty-year friendships

Generosity of spirit creates deep bonds that can carry well beyond the heat of battle. In November 2008, Terry Jefferson, a Black veteran of the Civil Rights Movement in her eighties, was living in a subsidized rental in Newark, New Jersey. Her health was deteriorating, especially because of problems with diabetes. One day she collapsed and was rushed to a hospital where they regulated her insulin and did a complete work-up to analyze her many physical problems. A week later, the hospital transferred her to a rehabilitation center for what Terry thought would be a few weeks. But as the weeks passed, Terry realized there was no plan to release her. The next thing she knew, her apartment complex evicted her.

But Terry was not alone. She had lifelong friends and comrades fighting for her. They stuck with her for eighteen months, advocating for her with the hospital, with lawyers, and with apartment managers until the hospital released her and her apartment building took her back. Three friends—Carol Glassman, Steve Block, and Junius Williams—had known her since 1964, when they had worked together in the same Civil Rights Movement project called the Newark Community Union Project (NCUP). Forty years ago, they were activist students who had come to organize in Newark, and Terry headed up the "community" welcome committee.

NCUP was based in the predominantly Black South Ward and the virtually all Black Central Ward of Newark, New Jersey. It was an alliance between "community people," who were already in battles against their slum landlords, and "the students," who were college-educated and came from the outside to help organize. NCUP organized rent-strikes, campaigns against police brutality, and electoral insurgencies of the Freedom Ticket, a third-party movement in which community people ran for public office, including Terry Jefferson, who ran for state assembly. NCUP also played a pivotal role in the election of Kenneth Gibson, the first Black mayor of Newark.

In the NCUP storefront, Terry was the office manager and den mother for the younger organizers who were new to the project. Carol, Steve, and Junius were among them. Terry went every day to Randy's Meat Market on Clinton Avenue to buy bologna, American cheese, white bread, and mustard—

our favorite (and cheapest) lunch at the time. Terry opened her home to the students, made great fried chicken, and taught the newcomers how to imitate her unique recipe. She made sure all the students had housing in the same apartment buildings in which the community lived. She, along with Jesse Allen, who was later elected as a Newark city councilman, and Louise Patterson, a compassionate militant, were the welcoming and orientation committee for students and community people alike. Terry's generosity of spirit made her the community anchor for the entire project.

Deeply influenced by the organizing of the Student Nonviolent Coordinating Committee in the South, NCUP was a model of Northern civil rights organizing and was emulated by many organizers in the north. NCUP's story was captured in the documentary film *Troublemakers,* by Norman Fruchter, Robert Machover, and Robert Kramer. Student organizers Carol Glassman and Steve Block were among the most dedicated members. Even after NCUP disbanded, they moved to the nearby Ironbound district of Newark to organize working-class whites to fight their class exploitation and ally with the Black community. They left Newark in the 1970s; Carol moved to New York City to be a therapist, and Steve moved to Upstate New York to participate in local politics. They more than anyone stayed in close touch with the Newark community leaders and continued their ties through birthdays, funerals, new jobs, arrests, drug rehabilitation, adoption, and financial support—whatever it took to help.

When Terry was admitted to the hospital in 2008, Carol and Steve, with the help of Junius Williams, now a civil rights attorney, jumped to her side. When the rehab facility would not release her, they launched a yearlong fight with the manager. They argued that Terry had recovered both physically and cognitively and could live on her own. Then they hired a lawyer who represented Terry. They sent out e-mail appeals to NCUP alumni, who gladly helped with the expenses of the campaign. They had a breakthrough after a year when the rehabilitation home appointed a new director, who became an advocate for Terry in alliance with the staff gerontologist, who declared her able to live on her own if she could get help regulating her diabetes medication.

For eighteen months, Carol and Steve talked to each other daily about Terry and kept in close touch with her granddaughter ReRe. In an April 2010 fund-raising appeal to NCUP alumni (whom she called "Dear Adopted Jeffersons"), Carol delivered the "almost getting to the finish line" news.

> So finally we have some movement. An apartment is available in the building that Terry has lived in for so many years and where she wants to return; but she has no furniture. The nursing home crowd has agreed she can live in the community as long as there are arrangements to test and adjust her blood-sugar levels. Sometimes it feels like a full-time job. If I kept notes and could bear to go over this process, it [would be] an indictment of the entire welfare system.

In May 2010, Carol's next dispatch arrived.

> Dear Gang, So the end is in sight. We have solved the last problem with the help of a nurse I found accidentally who I'll call Saint Susan. She runs a private project that provides skilled aides who can check Terry's diabetes levels so the last obstacle has been overcome.

And in June 2010, Terry, now eighty-seven, moved back to the apartment to a great welcome from the tenants who considered her a friend and "organizer." Steve rented a U-Haul, Carol's sister arranged for a web-based donation of furniture, and Terry is now securely in her Newark apartment on South Orange Avenue "with a view of New York to die for," as Carol describes it.

In the midst of the deterioration of the social welfare state that the organizers in the 1960s had worked so hard to expand, poor people are often left alone to deal with "personal" problems that are deeply political—as they bear the blows of society's abandonment of Black and Latino communities and the urban and rural poor. In this case, there was a happy ending because three relentless organizers with many allies had learned their lessons well, and had the generosity of spirit to match that which Terry had shown them.

In a fitting coda, Terry's granddaughter ReRe, a young child when we all knew her in the 1960s, is now in her forties with seven children of her own and living in the Bronx. She is Terry's main support and commutes to take care of her at least once a week. ReRe told Carol that whenever she gets discouraged about life she goes to the New York Public Library and watches a copy of *Troublemakers*. It helps her remember where she came from, and cheers her up and gives her hope.

Self-Sustaining:
Takes Good Care of Himself

It takes energy, drive, and will to do the transformative organizer's job over a lifetime. Even for the most dedicated it is a constant struggle. Organizing is hard, stressful work, with long, irregular, and unpredictable hours. It requires an organizer able to deal constantly with the political, class, racial, gender, cultural, and personal contradictions among the diverse people with whom she works daily. The new organizer dreams of an idyllic organization, only to discover that there are many tensions among the members that have to be addressed, and the organizer's role as group builder is stressful. Even those who love to work with others (and organizer is the ultimate "social" job) have days when the weight of organizational life makes them want to be alone.

Many of the best organizers work full-time in factories, offices, schools, and hospitals, doing forty hours or more a week on their "regular job" while they organize coworkers during breaks and lunches. Then they go to the office of their primary movement organization where they carry out union-organizing drives, campaigns to protect abortion clinics, and demonstrations to defend immigrants facing deportation.

Over time, the work becomes more manageable as your skill level rises. But just as you grasp one level of activity, the organization drives the pace faster and sets the goals higher —just like our adversaries do. After all, history calls us forward into the struggle for social justice, and there is so much work to do. Under this increasing demand, each organizer confronts a critical point of transformation—the test of herself.

Burnout is a real concern. So is going through the motions, quitting on the work without realizing you are doing it. To survive and succeed, each organizer must cultivate an ever-evolving tactical plan to ground himself—to sustain and nourish himself as a long-distance runner. Perhaps the most important requirement is to feel grounded in the purpose of your life, the meaning and significance you attach to your choices, your self-identity. You must know why you are an organizer and why self-care is not self-cultivation but a necessary part of the life of an organizer who wants his work to make a difference.

Many modalities and resources can be helpful. There are athletic activities such as working out, running, and team sports; creative activities such as dance, writing, drawing; spiritual practices and traditions rooted in the histories of our communities; and a tremendous variety of wellness and healing practices ranging from food and diet regimens to massage, counseling, acupuncture, and energy healing. There are institutions, centers, and retreats all over the country dedicated to many of these practices and traditions.

As each organizer explores and builds her path to self-care and healing, she undertakes a lifelong study of her own body, mind, and spirit. What are my limits, what makes me sick, what is toxic to me, where do I need healing? What nourishes me, heals me, sustains me, rejuvenates me? Transformative organizers develop a deep understanding that answering these questions is essential for their viability over the long haul. There are people who "burn themselves out" and blame "the movement." Upon further examination, one often finds that either their organization or the person's own practice was not guided by a plan for long-term viability. With room for rest and reflection, a constant exposure to the injustices of the system, and perhaps building a more sustainable organization, "burn out" need not be a fatal condition.

The role of rest

There will always be periods—sometimes for long stretches—when fighting to win a campaign demands long hours and stressful work. There are moments of struggle—when the pace is intense and you are in the leadership—when you realize that you have to be creative to make sure you still find time during the day for meditation, exercise, and relaxation. But over the long haul, balancing the work with enough rest and personal time is essential. It's critical for organizers and long-distance runners to model behaviors for others that demonstrate you can be a dedicated revolutionary and a good father, mother, son, daughter, brother, sister, friend, and comrade. It is possible and necessary to have a great work ethic and also keep yourself in excellent mental, physical, and spiritual shape from taking an early weekday walk on your favorite path to a weekend trip to the mountains or a weekend training in meditation.

On the intensive side, there are retreats for organizers all over the country where you can spend weeks for self-directed healing, writing, introspection, rest, relaxation, or rejuvenation—anything but the work you left behind. Vallecitos Ranch in New Mexico is particularly dedicated to movement people, as is the Windcall Institute, which provides two- to four-week modules for rest, relaxation, and meditation for movement organizers. There is also the Alston/Bannerman Fellowship, which gives sabbaticals to movement veterans of color. Social Justice Leadership does group training to integrate transformative exercises that address the pain of internalized oppression. Organizers will also design restorative trips and journeys on their own for vacations or time off.

Then there are the forms of rest and rejuvenation we integrate into our daily lives. It might be keeping your weekly "date night" with your partner. Or making sure that, no matter how many evening assignments you have, some nights are protected for cooking healthy food and having dinner with friends or family, especially if you have young children. Organizers should make regular time for the things they love to do—athletic, artistic, social, spiritual—that foster a deep connection between body and spirit, physical and mental, human being and the earth. Watching great films in theaters or at home is a combination of escape and rejuvenation. Other times, organizers have told me that they had a great weekend "just being a homebody, doing my laundry" and all the other simple, centering things that create a sense of order and peace at home so that you feel ready to get back into battle. We should not underestimate the profound value of rest for the mind and body—the beauty of doing nothing.

Taking care of cadre

No organizer can take good care of herself without the support of her organization. The best transformative organizations integrate the care of organizers into their collective life and encourage organizers, as a matter of strategy and humanity, to take good care of themselves.

During the 1960s, the women's movement took leadership on the theory that "the personal is political" and paid great attention to relationships in the home between women and women, women and men. It encouraged women to lead lives of political activism and of self-care and self-respect. *Our Bodies, Ourselves,* by the Boston Women's Health Book Collective, was a great contribution to women's healing and medical advice and reflected a far more integrated approach to mind/body work than was available at the time.

Throughout the 1970s, the psychiatrist R. D. Laing urged a separation of psychotherapy from the medical institutions of psychiatry. To collectivize the process of dealing with trauma as a political question, a movement called Radical Psychiatry held clinics and drop-in centers, invoking the mantra "change not adjustment," and challenged the system's belief that mental health meant going along with the system's program. Franz Fanon, a psychiatrist in Algeria and the author of *The Wretched of the Earth*, studied the psychopathology of colonization. He taught the revolutionary movement that only the rebellion of the oppressed against the colonial oppressor could heal the pain of the oppressed and reconstruct their personalities for the better after centuries of internalized oppression. Augusto Boal, the Brazilian revolutionary and founder of the Theater of the Oppressed, made a breakthrough in participatory theater in which "the audience" became the actors. After many years of doing agitprop plays, which broke the plane between actors and audience, and involving working people in the political performing arts, Boal became concerned about the internalized oppression that held social movements back. After many years of fighting the cop in the streets, Boal led an international movement theater practice aimed at busting "the cop in the head," that is, challenging the taboos and self-restricting psychological dynamics that prevent people from being the fullest and most effective versions of themselves. Another approach is what is called "body work," which proliferated as organizers sought to break the back of internalized oppression and integrate many healing techniques used around the world.

Third World revolutionary organizations in the United States also developed elaborate, collectivized child-care systems. Parents with children knew they could drop their children off for clean, well-organized child care at each other's homes with actual curriculum, games, and rest. They knew that every member of the organization, whether they had children or not, took a regular turn as part of the child-care system.

In the best movement organizations, births, marriages, illnesses, and funerals are a normal part of the life cycle and are addressed in a collective way. More often than not, in low-income organizations people take up collections to help for funerals, new babies, people who lose their jobs or are threatened with eviction.

Today, as throughout history, many people of all ages are confronted with the opportunity and obligation to become caregivers when their family members or close friends suffer serious illnesses that the "private" health-care system cannot accommodate. Organizers with those responsibilities need more flexible hours as well as collective assistance and support in seeking the best solutions possible. Those who take care of others must be cared for by friends and comrades, and given some time to take care of themselves.

In such situations, I have been approached by staff and members of my organization who say, "I am worried about so and so. She looks exhausted, is nervous, and at times loses her temper; she seems overburdened and needs some help." I immediately approach that person to see how we can be of help. Often the best solution we come up with is a reduced workload and some time off for reflection, rest, and relaxation.

Today, our society has been stripped of many of the social services won in the past and we are very far from achieving the socialization of care-giving labor that is now left to the nuclear family, primarily women, to absorb. Central to the aims of our long-term struggle are universal social welfare, health care, and caregiving.

Yet, while struggling for these visions of a future social system, collectivity is necessary now. It is very difficult for a successful organizer to take care of herself if she is not in an organization that takes care of its people and supports practices of self-care. It's also very hard to take a real rest without being able to trust in your organization to carry on the work and on your coworkers to carry out your assignments.

From within the work itself

A transformative organizer knows that the foundation for sustainable practices—for life, health, spirituality, family, relationships to their comrades and friends—is loving one's work. As the scientist and socialist Albert Einstein observed, we should lead our lives based on "the satisfaction of the desires and needs of all, as far as this can be achieved, and achievement of harmony and beauty in the human relationships."

If you don't like the work, if you aren't a dedicated fighter who gets true joy from the struggle, if you don't agree with the Movement Building project, no amount of breaks, healing, therapy, yoga, recreation, or motivational interventions will save you from dropping out and abandoning the challenge of transforming society.

Transformative organizers know a most precious truth: that much of the deepest healing, transformation, and rejuvenation comes from within the work itself. Organizing is not alienated labor. We thrive on the collectivity of the work: we are inspired by the deep satisfaction and meaning of struggling with each other and being struggled with, singing together, chanting together, fighting shoulder to shoulder and changing society.

The healing and rejuvenation that we find within the work of organizing, and the healing and rejuvenation that we pursue outside the work of organizing, are not the same. One cannot substitute for the other. But they are also not separate. They are deeply connected and mutually interdependent. Successful organizers take good care of others and take good care of themselves.

Completes the Circle:
From Start to Finish

The successful organizer over time becomes a lead organizer, a senior organizer, and through practice, study, and observations comes to understand all the tasks involved in carrying out a job from beginning to end—"completing the circle." Through rigorous training and self-improvement, the successful organizer can either do all of the jobs required, or can find and organize people who can carry out the specific tasks that he can't. At the highest level of training and leadership, an organizer is able to function as a microcosm of the entire organization, capable of generating entire campaigns, from strategy to tactics, from the highest level of theory to the most minute level of detail.

Many organizers-in-training and even experienced organizers struggle with their job, which often feels bigger than they can handle. One solution is to simplify the job description and task load, making hard choices to reduce the level of responsibility and make the circle smaller. For whether the task is big or small, you still have to be able to complete it from start to finish. The senior organizers are grappling with the whole of a campaign or even the entire organization.

They supervise less-experienced organizers, whom they ask to pick up a piece of the puzzle, which is often challenging enough in itself.

When I say in complimenting an organizer that "she can complete the circle," I mean that you can give her an assignment and she will grasp the entire process, do a lot of original thinking about how to solve all the problems involved in the job, and bring the task or campaign to a successful conclusion. You can tell, just as in training an athlete, a dancer, or a musician, when the student has the awareness. You can feel the transition from grappling with a problem to having the confidence and consciousness to solve it.

The key to organizational growth is expanding the leadership team—a group of people who can head up an entire piece of the operation and do the job from beginning to end. Sometimes an organization has an explosive growth of secondary leaders, those who when given strong supervision can make major breakthroughs in the work. But the organization can't initiate new projects, new campaigns, new forms of organizations until there is a core of the most qualified leaders to head them up.

Mark Masaoka and Eric Mann:
How cadre turned an auto factory on its head

At the General Motors Van Nuys plant in California, from 1981 to 1987, I worked very closely with another comrade, Mark Masaoka. We worked on the assembly line along with five thousand other workers making the Chevrolet Camaro and Pontiac Firebird. We were shop-floor organizers and militants in the United Auto Workers. Mark developed very close ties to workers of all nationalities but in particular to the Black workers in the hot-as-hell body shop where he worked. I worked in "hard trim," where we completed the instrument panels before the cars' dashboards, seats, and upholstery were installed.

In 1982, during the age of plant closings, GM announced

a layoff of the entire second shift—the 2,500 lower-seniority workers. In the past, mass layoffs would be cushioned by the supplementary unemployment benefits (SUB), a union-won benefit paid by the company on top of our unemployment insurance. But by 1982, there had been so many layoffs and plant closings in recent years that the SUB fund was running low, and the lower-seniority workers would qualify for the fewest benefits.

Mark and I and a few higher-seniority workers in the union's Political Action Committee developed a plan to respond to the crisis in a way to avert the layoffs. If we could get the higher-seniority workers to agree, the union would demand that the company run the plant on two shifts, four days a week, without any overtime. That reorganization would reduce production by at least 20 percent to deal with declining sales, without necessitating mass layoffs. Some of the higher-seniority workers did not agree with the plan. They felt they had won their seniority and had the right to five days of work and, with the second shift laid off, perhaps the right even to make overtime when short-term demand pushed the company to make extra cars without having to call the second shift back.

Mark and I consulted with our union president, Pete Beltran, who said he supported the idea, but as an elected official he could not afford to anger the higher-seniority workers of the first shift. He wanted us to demonstrate that there was significant support from first-shift workers before he would risk his neck (and reelection). We also agreed that the union had to be careful not to jeopardize hard-fought seniority rights. Thus, the plan couldn't work unless the higher-seniority workers endorsed it.

Mark and I wrote up a leaflet arguing that sharing the burden would be the greatest form of union solidarity and would keep five thousand of us working. We developed an organizing team of a dozen active workers to circulate the petitions and for two days used every break, every lunch hour, and time before and after each shift to get workers to sign the petitions. In the end, fifty workers circulated petitions and more than five hundred signed them.

The second night we had to move fast because the layoff was imminent. We went back to my house at two in the morning, after our work on the swing shift was over. On an IBM Selectric typewriter, we wrote one master letter to the company that consolidated all the names we'd gathered from the dozens of petitions that had been circulated at the plant. I typed as Mark worked to decipher whether a signature was for Pedro or Pablo, Gonzalez or Gomez. Finally, at 6:00 a.m., we finished. I crashed while Mark took the final copy to a printer who was waiting for it with a rush order. Then he went home to grab a few hours of sleep. I got up at 10:00 a.m. and got to the printer by noon, where the leaflets were ready just as we had planned. I took them to the GM plant by 1:00 p.m. I met with a dozen workers in front of the entrance to the plant who were in on the organizing plan. We distributed it to swing-shift workers who began to trickle into the plant before the 3:30 p.m. shift and distributed a thousand more copies of the flyer to the day-shift workers as they left the plant at 3:00 p.m. Mark met me at the union hall, grabbed his share of the leaflets, and we went into the plant to work another eight hours on the assembly line and distribute the flyers to more workers at every break and lunch.

In twenty-four hours, we had turned the workers' organizing and petitions into a flyer distributed to union president Pete Beltran, the union's executive board, and the entire factory of five thousand workers. Many high-seniority workers had joined our movement. It impressed everybody who had signed the petitions that they had gone home from work and somehow, by the time they returned to work sixteen hours later, there was their name as part of a flyer. They had some sense that "somehow," as if through magic, some dedicated shop-floor organizers had generated the multiplier effect on each other's work and completed the circle.

With that level of support, Pete brought GM to court to oppose the entire layoff on the grounds it created irreparable harm and violated the union contract. We won a temporary restraining order, which was big news: "UAW Local Stops GM from Laying Off Workers." But the decision was quickly overturned by a higher court. Still, the level of class consciousness and solidarity we created through the campaign was a major boost to our longer-term strategy of keeping GM Van Nuys open, and it increased Mark's and my standing in the eyes of the workers. Increasingly, workers were seeing that the Left was a real asset to the union and realizing that their involvement in the union's efforts to challenge the company was their only hope of keeping their jobs.

Mark and I had mastered every element of the job and completed the circle—we carried off the campaign from conception to execution. At every level of work, each organizer has to master the job as a whole, whether large or small, that is in front of them. Completing the circle is both philosophical and tactical—there is a growing sense of mastery that comes with practice, diligence, and experience.

Tactically Agile: Masters the Decision of the Moment

There are great strategists and tacticians who can navigate the ship in the storm, find the long-term direction of the campaign, and make decisions that can take days or even weeks to make, allowing time for collective discussion, reflection, and back-and-forth debate. Then there are other decisions that have to be made in a matter of minutes, sometimes seconds. These decisions are often made in the heat of battle by the lead tactician, the lead organizer, who has to think on his feet and make irrevocable choices. To remain agile in these situations, an organizer must always remember that things rarely go according to plan. But one can't just throw caution to the wind: as the French chemist Louis Pasteur observed, "Chance favors the prepared mind."

Organizers come to master the decision of the moment through training and preparation. The best have a lot of experience at decision making in high-stakes settings, have a good grasp of the organization's tactical objectives going into battle, and have studied history so as to gain a broad understanding of almost all the moves that are possible. They have internalized key tactical parameters that the organization has codified (such as, "Never attack your opponent personally," or, "Never burn bridges, even if they do."). They are rigorous with scenario planning ("If x happens, we do y.")—thinking through the many different potential tactical calls, not to pre-determine every decision, but to unlock the mind from a rigid commitment to any single path.

Bob Travis thinks on his feet during the Flint Sit-Down Strike

The Great Sit-Down Strike of the United Auto Workers in Flint, Michigan, stands out among the militant union organizing drives of the 1930s, with Flint's workers defeating the capital-ists in what was acknowledged as "the strike heard round the world." This was a turning point in the long battle for indus-trial unions, which lead to the mass unionization of the auto, steel, rubber, electronics, and mining industries, and virtu-ally every other manufacturing job.

In 1936, the UAW organizers at Flint were trying to ne-gotiate a contract for all autoworkers with the ferociously anti-union General Motors. The objective was to force GM to recognize the UAW as the bargaining agent for its employees—one of the most radical ideas of its time. Manage-ment's weapon against a traditional strike—when workers walk out and withhold their labor power—was to use scabs to replace the striking workers, especially the most militant ones, and never rehire them. This was a powerful threat given the mass unemployment of the Great Depression. Although their usual tactics had been thwarted by GM's strategies, the workers were tactically agile enough to devise a new plan for a strike. They seized upon a new tactic of a "sit-down" strike. Workers would not only refuse to work but would occupy the plants, sleeping in the factory and preventing any work from being done until the company recognized the union.

The team of Robert Travis and Wyndham Mortimer were the acknowledged lead organizers of the United Auto Workers. On December 30, 1936, they initiated a sit-down strike at GM

Fisher Body #1, in Flint, a plant that was critical to the entire GM system. It made the dies, the metal molds that stamped out the body parts for Buick, Pontiac, and Oldsmobile. No dies, no parts. No parts, no cars. No cars, no profits for GM.

At first, only a few workers were occupying Fisher Body #1. In his book *Organize! My Life as a Union Man,* Mortimer describes what happened next (italics added).

> On December 29, 1936, the General Motors Corporation secretly began to remove important dies from Fisher #1. The purpose was to get them out of this union "hotbed." One of the workers on the night shift, John Ananich, called [Bob] Travis and said, "They are going to move the dies out, Bob!" Travis, *who was quick to make decisions,* told Ananich to get some of the other union men and to stop the dies from being moved. Travis then called the office girl . . . and told her to put the flicker on. . . . When it was on, it meant that something of importance was happening, so at lunchtime the workers came streaming across the street to the union hall.
>
> *The meeting was short and to the point.* Travis told them that the dies meant their jobs, and if they permitted the dies to be taken away, many of them would be unemployed. The workers decided to strike the plant, and to sit in and protect their jobs. *It was a crucial decision,* since if the workers went home over the weekend, and New Year's Day following, they would be leaving their jobs unprotected and the dies could be moved without opposition. The workers went directly from the meeting and took over the plant. They shouted from the windows . . . "She is all ours, Bob." . . . Thus began the historic forty-four-day sit-down strike.

The sit-downers were part of a larger group of workers who were striking but not occupying the building. In a tremendous display of tactical agility, the sit-downers in Fisher Body

#1 immediately began to organize the strike. They held an open and free election in which the workers elected Walter Moore as "mayor" of the plant with a council of ten people. The new mayor appointed his own police chief and asked the company police to leave the premises. The company police agreed, leaving the entire Fisher Body #1 plant controlled by the strikers. As Mortimer observed, "A Sanitary Engineer was appointed to see that everything was kept clean and orderly. It is widely accepted that the factory was kept cleaner and more orderly than it ever was before."

Over the next six weeks, Bob Travis, Wyndham Mortimer, Roy Reuther, Henry Krause, and other UAW leaders had to make rapid decisions every day in order to maintain the workers' control of the GM plants in the face of employer threats, injunctions, right-wing mobs, and two armed assaults by police that workers met with fire hoses and thrown auto parts. Against the constant threat of armed police raid, Bob Travis and the UAW leadership organized impressive community support for the workers that slowed the hand of the police. They were aided by key allies—Michigan governor Frank Murphy, who would not allow the police to forcibly eject the sit-downers, and President Franklin Roosevelt, who hated the right-wing automakers—Henry Ford, Walter Chrysler, and GM's Alfred P. Sloan—who had all campaigned against him.

On February 11, 1937, GM executives admitted defeat and signed an agreement recognizing the union. But the UAW leaders again demonstrated their tactical agility by seizing the moment and immediately initiating union-organizing drives in every GM factory across the country. By 1938, the UAW membership went from 30,000 to 500,000. They made history for hundreds of thousands of GM and UAW workers for the rest of the twentieth century.

Francisca Porchas takes on Mayor Villaraigosa

In 2006, the Strategy Center and Bus Riders Union had an organizing plan for the next meeting of the National Latino Congreso, the high-profile gathering of five hundred Latino elected officials, college faculty, professionals, social service agency staff, activists, and organizers. The mayor of Los Angeles, Antonio Villaraigosa, was to be a key speaker.

We went there with clear objectives: to increase our contacts and influence in the Latino community, to get the Congreso to support our Billions for Buses campaign, and, in turn, get Congreso delegates to pressure Mayor Villaraigosa to stop building rail, buy a thousand more buses, and lower bus fares.

We needed to show our initiative as an independent force within the Latino united front. Our initial plan was straightforward. The mayor would give his speech on his environmental record. Then, during the question-and-answer period, Francisca Porchas, a lead organizer of the Bus Riders Union, would put forth our program that the Congreso had endorsed and ask the mayor, in front of an audience that he saw as his, to change his position and immediately buy five hundred new buses on the road to one thousand.

The day before the mayor's address, we were told by Congreso leaders that he would not take any questions after his talk. He would give his speech on the environment and leave. We argued, as participants in the Congreso, that we had the political and moral standing in the city to allow us to make a statement from the floor on behalf of 500,000 bus riders, 50 percent of whom were Latino.

That night, Francisca Porchas, another lead organizer, Esperanza Martinez, and I had a long discussion of tactics. We decided it was in the best interest of the movement to challenge the mayor in front of the group. He could not be allowed to speak and run. He was inaccessible at the MTA meetings. If we could not challenge him here, where was the public ability to even talk to elected officials?

We did scenario planning and role playing and decided that Francisca would interrupt the mayor's speech as he moved toward his conclusion, creating an incident that would force people to take sides—what I call "splitting the room." This tactic would pressure the mayor by showing him that we had a significant portion of his Latino base on our side. Francisca would have to make the tactical calls on the spot, judging how and when to move in order to make the intervention before the mayor got away.

The next day, as anticipated, the mayor gave a long speech in which he portrayed himself as a champion of the environment but did not address any of the BRU's demands. In fact, he put forth programs that were directly contrary to ours. As he was about to say "in conclusion," Francisca chose her moment, stood up, and said, "Mr. Mayor, I respectfully disagree with your policies." At first, the mayor tried to ignore her, but she was relentless. "Mr. Mayor. Thank you. So will you stop the Red Line subway extension?" Her voice started out quivering, but her inner confidence and public persona grew with each sentence. "Will you buy five hundred new buses to start?"

Some members of the audience told her to sit down and shut up, some angry women sitting next to her were pulling on her arms, and local security guards approached, preparing to take her away. "Will you agree to reduce the bus fare?" she insisted. "Will you restrict the auto?" In challenging the rules, Francisca was carrying out civil disobedience and understood she was risking arrest. Yet she maintained her tactical agility and continued speaking while angry crowd members and police encircled her.

Finally, the mayor intervened out of decency and some empathy, saying, "Leave her alone. She has a lot of guts; she is doing her job. I was a community organizer, and I would have done just what she did." Then the mayor made a charismatic but hasty exit.

After the mayor left, the tide turned in the room. More than a hundred people came up to talk to Francisca and other BRU organizers. The entire place was buzzing with discussion. Some told her they "did not agree with her tactics" but admired her courage. Some wanted to know more about our Billions for Buses campaign. Even some who had told Francisca to sit down now told her they had supported her all the way.

Francisca's improvised performance had made history right on the spot. She had changed the balance of forces in the Latino united front represented in that room, shifting it decisively to the left. Already well-known, she had established herself as a major figure in the Los Angeles Chicano movement—a courageous young woman of Mexican parents representing the Bus Riders Union whose influence would carry over to many other public forums and meetings with elected officials.

And because Francisca was firm and respectful in her dealings with the mayor, and never made the struggle with the mayor personal, he was later an ally of the Bus Riders Union's in our efforts to stop fare increases and service cuts.

For Francisca, the Congreso events gave her greater confidence and tactical agility in front of the Los Angeles City Council, where she has been instrumental in passing a $23 million Bus Only Lanes project. She gained greater prominence as the lead organizer of the new national campaign, Transit Riders for Public Transportation. Her ability to seize the time, master the moment, think on her feet, and exhibit tactical flexibility hit all the right notes and is an asset to the organization to this day.

Organizers make their greatest leaps when they are put in charge of a task and given the responsibility to lead. When you are forced to master the decision of the moment, synapses in the brain that have never been used before explode into action—when you have to testify in front of a hostile governmental body, intervene in a heated dispute that erupts among organization members, put up posters on fences in the middle of the night with the possibility of police harassment or arrest, answer the press's questions representing the organization, or intercede in an argument on the bus. For the most committed organizers, these high-stress/high-reward situations are the key to their development. As the organizers develop more experience, learn from their mistakes, watch the work of people more developed, and as they read a lot of history and get back on the street to make more decisions, they will hear others observe, "She is a really creative tactician.

A Strong Class Stand:
Which Side Are You On?

During the Harlan County, Kentucky, coal miners' strikes of 1931, Florence Reese, a mother of seven, wrote a classic union song to inspire the miners to hold fast while the Pinkertons, a private police force in the service of the employers, were hunting down and trying to kill strikers, including her husband.

> Which side are you on?
> Which side are you on?
>
> My daddy was a miner,
> And I'm a miner's son,
> And I'll stick with the union
> 'Til every battle's won.
>
> Don't scab for the bosses,
> Don't listen to their lies.
> Us poor folks haven't got a chance
> Unless we organize.

Which side are you on?
Which side are you on?

Having a strong class stand means possessing political tough-
ness and a clear understanding that an organizer is on the
side of the working class against the corporate class, on
the side of the oppressed against the oppressors. An organizer with a strong class stand, then, is not at all exclusively,
a trade unionist affiliated with the U.S. labor movement.
Class stand is best reflected in the international class struggle, where working-class people in the United States support
the sovereignty and right to self-determination of Bolivia
and Venezuela, and call for the immediate withdrawal of
all U.S. troops, advisors, and mercenaries from Iraq and
Afghanistan.

Sometimes, finding your class stand is tested when the
system tries to threaten you, co-opt you, offer you bad compromises with a lot of flattery, or even (and this has happened
more often that you might think) offers you a good-paying job
to switch sides in the war. An organizer with a strong class
stand understands that she represents the interests of the
masses and will not fall victim to the false promises, seduc-
tions, and threats of the system.

A strong class stand is reflected in the young undocumented students who are committing civil disobedience and
risking arrest and deportation in Arizona and throughout the
United States to defeat reactionary immigration policies; in
the Domestic Workers United, which won a New York State
law giving domestic workers labor rights for the first time in
U.S. history; the rebellions of women held in slavery in traf-
ficking brothels in which they and young children are forced
into prostitution at the risk of their lives; and Iraq Veterans
Against the War, who have organized while they were in the
service and afterwards, despite strong military surveillance
and threats.

The Campaign to Keep GM Van Nuys Open:
A labor/community coalition takes on General Motors

During the mid 1970s through the 1980s and beyond, U.S. transnational corporations made a decision to export a lot of capital outside the country. It dramatically reduced its workforce and their benefits, and shut down a lot of plants—what was called the de-industrialization of America.

Some might have expected the powerful national unions to talk about "class struggle" and to effect a national policy to restrict plant closings. Instead, influenced by Reaganite free-market capitalism and out of desperation to keep what members they could, union leadership turned to a new theory of "labor-management cooperation." According to this theory, there is no need for the working class to struggle against the employers, because the interests of labor and management are the same. No longer adversaries, labor and management are now on the same side, "the company team." This rhetorical partnership was followed by another massive wave of shutdowns of viable auto plants with virtually no notice.

By 1981, union workers in California were frightened, disoriented, and unrepresented. Ford had closed its Milpitas-San Jose plant. Mack Truck and Goodyear Tires had shut down their California plants. And GM had permanently shuttered its Southgate plant in the heart of L.A.'s once-robust heavy industrial district. In that same year, GM management came to the Van Nuys workers in Los Angeles' San Fernando Valley and told us our only chance to save the plant was to embrace the "team concept": to work harder (as in, speed up the line, take more work on our jobs), "share in the sacrifice" (give up benefits), and convince U.S. consumers to "buy American" (attack Japanese imports). If we didn't embrace the "team concept," the consequence was clear. Our plant was on the endangered list.

No one took this lightly. Workers who had given GM fifteen to twenty years of their lives suddenly faced the prospect of having to look for other jobs. For most autoworkers, the factory was their home. They were proud of their work and, while it was a one-way love affair, very loyal to GM. And they knew—as all working people knew, especially people of color and women—that this was one of the best-paid working-class jobs left in a de-industrializing city. So, the workers, our union leadership, and our communities reached a crossroads. Should we trust that management was really on the same team with us in their plan to save the plant—or was it time to fight? It was Florence Reese's question once again, "Which side are you on?"

The debate was intense. But in the end, the workers of UAW Local 645 and its very progressive president, Pete Beltran, chose to fight, with me as the lead organizer of a new, controversial, high-stakes militant campaign: the Labor/Community Campaign to Keep GM Van Nuys Open. Our campaign would threaten GM with a boycott of its cars in L.A. if it moved to close the plant. Since all U.S. labor contracts prohibit workers from boycotting their own company, the key was to build the Labor/Community Coalition to Keep GM Van Nuys Open beyond the autoworkers. We needed churches, businesses, elected officials, student groups, and women's groups—especially those in the Black and Latino communities from which the majority of workers came—to join the coalition and give it the clout and the legal right to call and operate the boycott.

We spent two full years building that coalition into a powerful movement. Our highly publicized mass events, rallies, and marches were attended by many elected officials, clergy, and community leaders who pledged to support the boycott, including Cesar Chavez, Jesse Jackson, the actor Ed Asner, and the singer Jackson Browne.

Throughout the process of building the coalition and the campaign, the class stand of the workers, union leadership, and our allies was essential but was never a given. There were many key moments when our class stand was tested. One of the most decisive occurred as we turned the tide against GM.

In 1983, GM president James McDonald finally agreed—
through U.S. congressman Howard Berman's mediation
—to meet with our coalition at the Beverly Hilton Hotel. The
growth of our coalition over two years had made the threat
of our boycott real. McDonald gambled that he could back us
down in a face-to-face meeting. Our twenty-person delegation included Father Luis Olivares, Rev. Frank Higgins, State
Senator Art Torres, Assemblywoman Maxine Waters, Professor Rudy Acuña, Ed Asner, Rev. Ignacio Castuera, local president Pete Beltran, and a dozen more prominent community
leaders.

McDonald opened the meeting aggressively. His class
stand was clear. He lectured about GM's shrinking profits, the
growing Japanese competition. He said it was GM's right to
open and close plants as it saw fit. He asked us to drop our
talk of boycotts, and he began laying out his solutions to save
the plant: labor-management cooperation, worker givebacks,
and community tax breaks. As he continued, it became obvious that he had not come to negotiate or even to listen to us.

Finally, I stood up and interrupted him, "Mr. McDonald,
we heard your presentation. Out of respect for the twenty
community leaders in this room, I am asking you to please sit
down and let us make our presentation." The room was filled
with tension. McDonald initially refused and kept on talking. But he looked around the room at a group of militant and
prestigious community leaders, the majority of whom were
Black and Latino, whose expressions were signaling that, if
anything, I had been too polite. He sat down.

Coalition members asserted not only that GM's Van Nuys
plant was profitable, but that it had a responsibility to the
community and to the large workforce that was 50 percent
Latino, 15 percent Black, and 15 percent women. It would be
racist and sexist public policy to close the plant. Then, Rev.
Higgins told him that Black ministers loved Cadillacs, "but we
can learn to love Lincolns." Rudy Acuña, that father of Chicano studies, talked of the historic affinity of Chicanos to the

Chevy, but how our movement could break that connection in the Chicano market in L.A.—a county that was almost 50 percent Latino. The key to our leverage was that Los Angeles County, with ten million people, is the largest new car market in the United States.

Maxine Waters and Art Torres scolded McDonald for his condescending tone and told him that if he thought the boycott was a bluff, he should investigate the power of our coalition and our belief that we could cut GM sales by at least 10 percent in L.A. right off the bat. (As we later found out, McDonald had done just that. He had sent several Black employees as spies to investigate Rev. Higgins and the Baptist Ministers Conference. Apparently, they came back with a respectful assessment of our potential to carry out the boycott.)

To close our presentation, our chief negotiator, Maxine Waters (then an assemblyperson, now a member of Congress), pushed McDonald to drop his threats and make a commitment to the plant. "Do we have a commitment to keep the plant open for one year?" McDonald paused, and answered, "Yes." She asked, "Do we have a commitment for two years?" He again paused, and again agreed. When she got to three years, he said, "At that time we will have to make a decision about closing another group of plants, and I can't make a commitment beyond that."

After the meeting, Maxine Waters turned to me and said, "Well, what a learning experience. I introduce a bill in the legislature to require companies to give workers three months notice on a plant closing and my colleagues say it is too radical. And here, with a powerful grassroots coalition and a concrete threat we can carry out, we get him to promise to keep the plant open for three years. What do we learn from this story?" Rev. Higgins backed her up, saying, "When he walked in there, McDonald talked to us as if we were children. But when he walked out, he knew he had a tiger by the tail."

In that critical conversation, our strong class stand convinced GM president McDonald that ours was not the usual group of hat-in-hand union and community supplicants. He had no choice but to negotiate. As he told the press, after coming out of the meeting, "I don't like boycotts. I just don't think they're good for business."

Because of our work, GM kept the Van Nuys plant open for a full decade after it had threatened to close it. Thousands of GM workers kept their jobs, built up retirement credits, and many, having accrued ten more years of seniority, were able to transfer to other GM plants across the country once the plant was finally closed in 1992. Our coalition's collective class stand and tactical plan proved stronger than that of mighty General Motors. We knew which side we were on.

The Organizer as Expert:
Science in Service to the People

A successful transformative organizer has to lead with her politics of social transformation but also has to be knowledge-able in social facts, science, law, and the tactics of organizing. Today, if you want to go up against the system and actually fight to win, you have to know what you are talking about, study the science and the legal and legislative procedures in the many fields that apply, and learn a lot of different techni-cal skills to make you a successful organizer. Organizers must learn the committee structure of Congress and the atomic structure of the chemical 1,3-Butadiene, a known carcinogen. They must learn housing law, labor law, civil rights law, and environmental law. They must study urban planning, public health policy, and the science of climate change. They must learn to navigate the rules and procedures of the city council, the regulatory agency on their issue, and the United Nations.

Organizers who are ill-informed about their issues can speak only the general truths of the revolution and are out-matched by the scientists and expert witnesses marshaled by their opponents. They are usually unpersuasive, unable to effect actual change, and are used as caricatures by the system to discredit the movement. At the same time, activists or advocates who claim particular scientific or legal expertise but do not align with social movements and have no effective organizational strategy and tactics often miss the forward motion of social change and are easily manipulated by the system as "expert witnesses" for the establishment. You have to have good politics *and* good science.

Tom Goldtooth: *Indigenous rights on an international stage*

Tom Goldtooth is a prominent Native American organizer and the executive director of the Indigenous Environmental Network (IEN), with 250 independent affiliates in the U.S. As with all successful organizers, powerful historical and political forces shaped their development, as they all stand tall on the backs of their predecessors.

Tom grew up in the 1960s on a Navajo reservation in Arizona. His mother was the first Navajo woman to obtain a degree in microbiology, during the 1950s, and she later became chief medical technologist at one of the larger hospitals in Arizona. His stepfather was a conservative Navajo policeman. In the age of hippies, his father made sure that Tom would bear no resemblance—he would give him a buzz cut, "zip the sides and box it on top." Tom called it the "Bureau of Indian Affairs haircut." Tom attended Arizona State in the early '70s and was part of the Student Koalition of Indian Natives (SKIN). "I came to see the world through a Native-activism lens in the era of Native American resistance that was called the Red Power Movement," he said. It was a time when groups such as the National Indian Youth Council, United Native Americans, and the American Indian Movement (AIM) emerged as the leading force of Native insurgency, with Natives taking over San Francisco's Alcatraz Island for nineteen months, demanding ownership of the island and a Native university and museum. In 1972, Indians had a sit-in at the Bureau of Indian Affairs office in Washington, D.C., to challenge the racism and paternalism of the agency, and AIM rewrote history with its dramatic takeover of Wounded Knee, South Dakota, in 1973.

By late 1991, Tom had joined IEN and quickly moved through its ranks, first as a member of the national council, then as a national spokesperson, and later as its director. Through the encouragement of Winona LaDuke, an influential Ojibwe activist, he attended the First People of Color Environmental Leadership Summit, in Washington, D.C., to lend his voice to what Native Nations are experiencing in addressing environmental and economic justice issues.

As IEN grew, they won many cases of shutting down toxic- and radioactive-dumping proposals in Native lands by working with communities on the front lines of resistance. In the late 1990s, environmental health consciousness grew in the United States, with the reports of persistent organic pollutants (POPs) such as dioxin bio-magnifying and bio-accumulating in the environment, especially in the colder regions of the Arctic. POPs are the product of many industrial processes, paper mills, and the incineration of toxic waste. Once again, Native people were disproportionately affected by these toxic chemicals accumulating in their traditional foods and in the bodies and breast milk of Native women. This became a global problem, leading to the formation of a United Nations treaty-making initiative by governments of the world to negotiate an international legally binding agreement on the reduction and elimination of dioxin and eleven other chemicals from the environment.

Organizing around a rights-based approach, IEN looked for an international target and ways to use international pressure to support Indigenous rights and universal human rights, instruments to create political will among nation-states to agree to a global treaty to eliminate these chemicals. They had to integrate science, both Indian and Western, with political strategy and grassroots organizing among Native communities. Tom explained,

We wanted to make sure that we were balancing the importance of Indigenous traditional knowledge [ITK] along with Western science. Working with the Healthcare Without Harm Coalition, we were able to find doctors who had the expertise to do epidemiological studies to indicate these pollutants were widespread, dangerous, and showed up in significant numbers in the population studies—and who would work in a principled way with Native peoples.

The women of the St. Regis Mohawk Tribe developed a grassroots public-health research initiative called First Environment, which discovered that Mohawk women had high levels of PCBs in their breast milk. The campaign to address POPs issues in Native territories spawned a project to study the effects of toxic chemicals on Native populations in Canada within the eastern Great Lakes region. Hair, blood, and DNA samples were taken and tested to measure exposure levels to toxic chemicals.

When the Mohawk First Environment project investigated possible sources, they found that the PCB contamination was coming from the Reynolds Aluminum as well as General Motors plants, which have aluminum-processing plants and make automatic-transmission casings. It was discovered the bottom sediment of the St. Lawrence River was severely contaminated with PCB, poisoning the aquatic life. With the goal of raising knowledge and awareness across "Indian Country," IEN worked with many Native Nations and tribal grassroots groups—the St. Regis Mohawks in the eastern Great Lakes, the Gwich'in in Alaska, the Yukon in Canada, the Penobscot in Maine, and the Ojibwe in northern Minnesota—to design popular education materials and mobilize outreach plans to their communities. They explained, for example, how toxins function as endocrine disrupters that wreak havoc with the body's glands and hormones. IEN linked how these toxics negatively affect the treaty rights of the Native Nations to be able to fish, gather, and hunt clean and safe traditional foods.

As a result of this work, IEN argued for the importance of "speaking for ourselves," applying treaty rights and the rights of Indigenous Peoples at the local, national, and international level—a rebuke to some mainstream environmental groups who co-opt community demands and cut deals with the polluters against the best interests of communities of color. In 2000, IEN worked with the largest Native organization, the National Congress of American Indians (NCAI), to pass a resolution strengthening the work being done to reduce and eliminate these twelve POP chemicals. With NCAI support, IEN was able to apply the U.S. government-to-government relationship and put political pressure on the United States to act on its fiduciary and federal trust responsibilities to protect Native lands and its people.

During the IEN POPs campaign, Tom was chosen as the chief negotiator for the Indigenous delegation from North America, because he had the political acumen and scientific expertise that were needed for the job. He understood the role and mechanisms of the United Nations, the U.S. government, Native Nations, and the grassroots, including the long history of Native treaty relations. He knew the science, and he was immersed in the Native traditional knowledge and Native approach. He was able to inform, train, and organize a delegation on how to be effective and strategic in United Nations negotiations.

In 2001, in Stockholm, Sweden, the nation-states that were part of the convention on POPs signed the treaty to phase out and ban the twelve chemicals. To this day, with the strong lobbying of the chemical, plastic, and agricultural industries and other polluters, the U.S. Congress has not passed legislation to ratify the Stockholm POPs treaty, despite years of organizing by environmental and health groups,. Now, people in the United States, including the Native people and the broader population of vulnerable communities, do not have the protection of the international treaty.

On the positive side, the majority of countries have ratified the treaty, including those in the European Union and

China. And even though it has not signed the treaty, the U.S. government still must attend a Conference of the Parties, where every country must come before the United Nations to report on their progress or lack thereof on reducing PCBs in the water, soil, fish, and air.

In the UN, the Japan, U.S., Canada, Australia, and New Zealand bloc is called the JUSCANZ or "No" bloc because it opposes any form of international regulation of corporations. In that context, what IEN and Tom Goldtooth accomplished in this age of the cooptation of NGOs is very impressive. The Indigenous peoples of the United States along with Indigenous peoples throughout the world were an important force at the Stockholm conference and helped pass the treaty despite the opposition of the United States. Their participation validated a "rights based approach" to these international battles in which indigenous peoples argue for human rights that cannot be violated by the laws of nation states.

The next summit on Sustainable Development will be held in Rio de Janeiro, Brazil in 2012—called Rio + 20. Some of the IEN people were there in Rio in 1992, and Tom and a large delegation of IEN were in Johannesburg, South Africa in 2002, and will be there in Rio in 2012 where there will be a review of progress made of agreements that came out of Rio de Janeiro in 1992. As Tom observes, "These difficult battles are strengthened by a very long view that sees our role as protecting the present, the future, and the 7th generation to come."

Tom Goldtooth is committed to ensuring that the synthesis of indigenous and Western science with organized political power is taught to a new generation of environmental and spiritual warriors. "We have to bring our demands again and again, be very on point and strategic in picking our battles, and prepare the next generation to really take the battle on. The root cause of climate, environmental and economic injustice is an economic system that isn't sustainable. World leaders must develop a new economic paradigm that recognizes the Rights of Mother Earth."

Courageous and Militant:
On the Front Lines of the Battle

Anyone who has ever really struggled to change the system finds out about repression—and what it means to have the courage of his convictions. During the height of the labor movement, the song was "Which Side Are You On?" and the understanding was that miners or autoworkers would have to stand up to police, riot squads, and armed company goons. At the height of the revolutionary sixties, Eldridge Cleaver raised a challenge that became instant folklore: "You are either part of the solution, or you are part of the problem," and this was always accompanied by the challenge, "Are you willing to put your body on the line?" In one example, hundreds of young people risked their lives in Mississippi during the summer of 1964, knowing full well that the NAACP's Medgar Evers and CORE's Andrew Goodman, Mickey Schwerner, and James Chaney had been murdered before they arrived.

In 1964, the United States passed the Civil Rights Act, and in 1965, passed the Voting Rights Act. In 2008, Barack Hussein Obama was elected the first Black president of the United States. His election was built on the foundation of the courage of the thousands and millions of Black people who, through armed self-defense, nonviolent demonstrations met with billy clubs, and urban rebellions, finally won an end to Jim Crow and the right to vote. People made great sacrifices, sometimes giving their lives, for a cause that could not have been won without front-line organizers. It will take a new Civil Rights Movement to get any president to deal with the ravages of racism in the United States today. And, it will take a new generation of organizers to realize that the post-9/11 Office of Homeland Security will classify virtually any militant demonstration as "domestic terrorism." We need physical courage to bring our movements to the streets, knowing that the police retaliation may be quite severe.

Maria Guardado: Salvadorean saint

When the Strategy Center initiated the Bus Riders Union (BRU) in 1994, one of the key sources of our first grassroots members was the First Unitarian Church, a small, progressive church that offered sanctuary for the Salvadorean refugee community. From our outreach to that church, we had attracted several prominent Salvadorean activists who went on to play a prominent role in the BRU. Among them were Ricardo and Noemi Zelada and Maria Guardado—all of whom became named plaintiffs in The Labor/Community Strategy Center and Bus Riders Union v. Los Angeles MTA.

I had known Maria for many years and respected her relentless exposures of neoliberalism and her constant push for the BRU to play a stronger role in antiwar organizing. I later learned, through Witness: The Maria Guardado Story, a documentary by actor Randy Vasquez, that Maria was more of a hero than I even knew. In the film, Maria tells the story of how, as a young Catholic woman in El Salvador, she had been brought into the liberation movement by Archbishop Oscar Romero, the cleric who was murdered for his leadership of the democratic resistance. Many others were tortured and killed for their opposition to the U.S.-backed junta. Maria describes, slowly, each time gasping for air, how the military dictatorship sent troops to her house, kidnapped her, tortured and beat her, raped her. They broke her breastbone and backbone and left her for dead on the side of a road. She explains that during her torture she heard a man speaking in English and Spanish, that he was a U.S. "advisor" from the CIA, personally supervising her torture and near murder. After a very dangerous journey, Maria was able to come to the United States and get treatment in the Program for Torture Victims under the care of Dr. Jose Quiroga from Chile. She is now working with the Torture Abolition and Survivors Support Coalition International to help others who went through similar traumatic experiences.

After years of rehabilitation and post-traumatic stress that she still battles today, Maria began to get politically active again. She joined the Committee in Solidarity with the People of El Salvador (CISPES), and in 1994 joined the BRU at one of its first meetings. Maria has always said, "I am with the Bus Riders Union because the Strategy Center is providing an internationalist human rights perspective to that work." She talks to our members about the CIA, about the system, and is a passionate speaker at every BRU monthly meeting.

For most of us, who have more limited courage, hearing stories about people who have taken more risks and endured more sacrifice is a challenge to our own class stand, our own willingness to assume risk. The courageous example of individuals is critical, but courage must be found in a collective context, where the most successful organizers reflect a strategic and tactical courage. If you have ever been involved in a direct action sit-in, building takeover, or any other form of militant street protest, you become aware that what will happen to you is often beyond your capacity to predict—it depends upon the behavior of the police, or even hostile bystanders. Sometimes, even a sit-in hardly feels nonviolent when violent police armed with riot gear descend on you.

In any confrontation with the police, you go into battle with a knot in the pit of your stomach, fighting off fear that is usually dissipated, but not eliminated, by the militancy itself, the chanting, the commonality of the struggle, and the people on both sides of you taking the same risks. I remember an antiwar demonstration in Washington, D.C., in 1965. The police put us in a paddy wagon and then kept pushing more and more demonstrators into the wagon until we were stacked two deep without an inch to spare. They left us in there for five hours with the hot noonday sun beating down on the wagon. Some people panicked, felt they could not breathe. We talked each of us through it, that there would be (barely) just enough oxygen if we breathed slowly and did not panic. The group calmed itself into a collective embrace, but hour after hour we were very frightened. Finally, we were booked on misdemeanor charges and sent home on our own recognizance. They had already achieved their objectives, and many of us who were in that paddy wagon, such as folksinger Len Chandler, talk about that experience to this day.

Courage is best built and sustained in collective action and through an organization. It is hard to be courageous alone. It is your fellow workers, fellow community members, and fellow prisoners who can help you find just enough courage to do the job you have to do. And again, there must be a strategy that you believe in and a tactical plan that makes sense.

Sometimes, when I write about people far more courageous than I am, I wonder how I have been able to take the risks I have taken, and I still worry about the gap between my own courage and that which has been expected of and given by others. Courage, like most other qualities, can be learned, and must be built up one step at a time. In the end, you cannot fight for a transformative vision of society without being a successful organizer, and you can't be a successful organizer without at least a strong baseline of physical courage and the willingness to take risks and put your body on the line.

A Strong Work Ethic:
First to Arrive, Last to Leave

A ferocious work ethic is always a trait of successful organizers. A strong work ethic in the field of social movement organizing is often expressed in practice as "the first one to arrive and the last to leave." People who attract and retain members take pride in their work, take pleasure in their job well done, and work for their political collective as energetically as they would any family business or professional career opportunity. At every point, individual leadership requires modeling excellence and leading by example of dogged commitment. Often, this ethic calls for organizers to stay late to finish a job, put in extra hours to meet a deadline, and refuse to put off today's work until tomorrow. In many instances, successful transformative organizers test themselves by asking, "When do we leave?" and answering, "When the job is done."

When I worked as an auto assembler and coordinator of the Campaign to Keep GM Van Nuys Open, during every month of our nine-month layoff (during that entire period, we had no idea when and if we would ever be called back to work) we held a large Saturday meeting at the Union Hall in which the Community Services Committee distributed surplus food to the laid-off workers. We combined that with a planning meeting of the campaign, knowing it was the one time a month we could get so many workers, now scattered geographically, to come back to the union hall. More than a thousand laid-off GM workers came from all over Los Angeles County to get government food, including gigantic bars of a Velveeta-type cheese the workers called "welfare cheese." Many workers drove miles to get canned food and other necessities and had to ask the union for gas money to get home. It was hard for them to face that they were on welfare too.

Out of that group of a thousand, anywhere from two hundred to three hundred stayed for the two-hour meeting afterward to discuss the Campaign to Keep GM Van Nuys Open. We asked them to become community organizers, to take the campaign to their churches, other unions, and neighbors. Our tactics included high-visibility mass rallies with media coverage as well as smaller events, like Tupperware parties, barbeques, and extensive outreach to churches, to mobilize community support *before* the plant actually closed. A pivotal tactic was a massive letter-writing campaign to top GM management in Detroit from supporters who pledged to boycott the company if it did not keep the plant open.

Letter writing and mailing had become a central task in the organizing campaign, so we asked these members to stay to help with a mass mailing of 2,500 pieces to our laid-off members, urging their participation in an upcoming rally. Together, we put stamps and stickers on envelopes, sorting them by zip codes. Some people brought their families and thought it was fun. While most stayed for an hour or so, in the end it was the dozen most committed members who finished, knowing this task had to be worked on until it was completed. As the few of us sat stuffing the envelopes to the end of the day, I felt a sense of solidarity when several committee members commented, "I'm glad we're here together. Members need their government surplus food, their gas money, and their particular problems addressed. They need to see the union working for them. Plus, when we drop the mail bags at the post office, we know the job is done, and tomorrow we can move to the next step." It reinforced my understanding that being the first to arrive and the last to leave is an important element of winning the confidence of the people with whom you work and is often essential to getting the job done right. And as history would show, our strong work ethic was a critical component in the victorious Campaign to Keep GM Van Nuys Open.

National School for Strategic Organizing

The National School for Strategic Organizing (NSSO) is a six-month residency program for organizers in training (OITs), run for the past twenty years by the Strategy Center. NSSO has recruited more than a hundred organizers in training and graduated about ninety of them. More than a dozen graduates are working as staff for the Strategy Center, as virtually every staff person is a graduate of the school. It has turned out another thirty people living and working with the Strategy Center in Los Angeles as public school teachers and graduate students, and another twenty-five who have gone on to social-change work with other excellent organizations such as POWER (People Organized to Win Employment Rights) and Causa Justa::Just Cause in the San Francisco/Oakland Bay area and several Service Employees International Union locals throughout the United States.

Early in our history, we recruited OITs through a national search. Through a competitive essay process and extensive interviewing, we recruited some great people. But we did make some mis-assessments of people, which became almost immediately apparent. The OITs are required to arrive at the office every day no later than 8:45 a.m. They are then briefed about the day's objectives on the bus, which team they will be with and which bus. Sometimes a new leaflet has been produced that needs to be explained and clarified. Ninety percent of the organizers-in-training do just that, but we have had instances when a few OITs did not respect the urgency of being on time. They wandered in sometime between 9:00 and 9:30, always with an excuse and often, when criticized, reacted with defiance, as if they were being oppressed by their lead organizers A few thought they would set their own hours and make their own rules. A few have had to leave the program.

Now, we only accept organizers-in-training who have already interned or worked with us for months, because within a few weeks you can tell if someone has the commitment to do the job. Getting up early, coming in prepared, doing the job with skill and enthusiasm, and finishing it with a good attitude are attributes that always lead to success. We have never lost a person who was first to arrive and last to leave. Often, when organizers tell me that they are discouraged about the slow results of their work, how few members are coming in for the hours put in, I tell them, "Until you can get better results, why not put in more hours." Sometimes organizing is not about charisma or tactical brilliance; it's about putting in more time.

The everyday experience of Barbara Lott-Holland, a decade-long cochair of the Bus Riders Union, is an indication of why she is a successful organizer. Her work ethic, in both the private and movement sectors, is her calling card. She gets up at 5:00 a.m. to ride a bus to a job in the accounts receivable department of a law firm. Every Wednesday night, the Bus Riders Union holds a meeting of its planning committee, a dedicated leadership body of fifteen members and staff who plan the direction of the organization. Together they devise the critical path of the BRU's campaign for transportation equity. Barbara finishes work by 4:00 p.m. and then takes the long series of buses to get to the Strategy Center by 6:00. We begin each meeting at 6:30, have dinner together, and try to finish dinner and clear the table by 7:15.

Barbara then goes over the agenda and makes sure that other items carried over from past meetings are put on the table again. We usually end at 10:00 or 10:30, and often Barbara, conveying the joy that comes with a job well done, asks the group to extend the meeting to 11:00 or later if urgent actions are needed.

After the meeting is adjourned, I drive Barbara home to South L.A., and we talk for the half hour, about health, aging, diet, exercise, TV shows, usually anything but the work, but sometimes, yes, the work is so compelling or issues at the meeting not fully resolved that we keep discussing those issues. Often when we say good night, Barbara will say, "See you tomorrow!" and somehow we are both happy. Barbara is exhausted, facing five hours sleep, but she is not complaining. This is her job, and it's what gives her life the most meaning.

The most successful people in all fields have a great work ethic. The love of our work is essential, for we can't find a sustainable life if we find the political work unfulfilling and always seek escape from its rigors. In order to be successful organizers, we must work hard and take great joy in doing a job well from beginning to end.

Relentless:
Won't Take No for an Answer

For every successful organizer, in every successful organization, being relentless is essential. Being relentless means never giving up, pursuing your adversary through thick and thin, through short-term victories and defeats, so that every time the forces far more powerful than your movement look up, over, or back, there you are.

In virtually every instance—the Student Nonviolent Coordinating Committee versus the Ku Klux Klan; the Students for a Democratic Society and Black Student Union taking over Columbia University; the Battle in Seattle against multinational giants; the food security movement against DuPont, Dow, Monsanto, and Archer-Daniels-Midland—the movement is up against the most powerful forces, so powerful at times that the "conventional wisdom" is that political engagement is hopeless. Throughout history, it is the leaders and organizations that operate for years and decades on a campaign and do not abandon it that have the best chance, the only chance, to win. They generate leaders who are always coming up with new tactics, "fight, fail, fight again." It is only those organizations and organizers who are relentless, sustain their campaign, stick like glue to their adversaries, constantly probe their enemy's weaknesses that pull off transformative victories that even in retrospect seem miraculous.

Margene Bullcreek and the OGD

The nuclear energy industry is a dirty industry, known for the Three Mile Island, Chernobyl, and Fukushima disasters but equally dangerous because the "spent" nuclear rods are highly radioactive and no one wants them buried on their land—they are lethally radioactive forever. The nuclear power industry and the federal government have historically viewed Native American reservations, especially in Utah and Nevada, as "human sacrifice zones"—test sites for nuclear weapons, nerve gas, and a host of toxic and lethal human experiments. It is not surprising that the industry continues its practice of environmental racism by looking to these lands to dispose of nuclear waste. Needless to say, middle- and upper-class communities do not want radioactive waste anywhere near their world, so attention has long focused on the "sacrifice zones." Without sacrifice zones, the dangerous methods of nuclear production would have to stop.

In 1987, the federal government initiated the Office of the U.S. Nuclear Waste Negotiator to convince Indigenous peoples to accept a "temporary monitored retrievable storage site" for high-level nuclear waste on their land. The so-called negotiator targeted hundreds of tribes but could not get one to agree. An upsurge in Indigenous organizing was already succeeding in blocking waste from their lands. During the mid-1980s, Rufina Marie Laws led a movement to reject nuclear dumping on the Mescalero Apache Reservation in Arizona and Grace Thorpe, founder of the National Environmental Coalition of Native Americans, built a successful resistance movement on the Sauk and Fox reservation in Oklahoma. Margene Bullcreek, a member of the tiny Skull Valley Goshute Indian Tribe in Utah, recalls becoming involved in 1990 "when I read there was a study to place 'temporary monitored retrievable storage' on our land. Every site picked was an Indian reservation; no one else wanted the danger no matter how much they were paid." She began to organize resistance when Private Fuel Storage (PFS), an industry consortium, spent $300,000 to send members of several tribes to Great Britain and Japan to convince them that "nuclear waste is safer than a microwave."

The concept of "temporary" storage was a manipulation from the start based on the "promise" that the hazardous material would later be moved to a permanent site. But who would monitor the possible accidents, and once they were there, who could decide if they were retrievable if no one else wanted them? Indigenous peoples know very well that such promises are made to be broken. They did not want the nuclear waste on their reservations, temporarily or permanently. Their history had taught them that they had to be relentless in their resistance.

By 1992, the U.S. Congress accepted defeat with its ploy of a nuclear waste negotiator and cut all funding for the program—apparently nobody wanted to negotiate a nuclear future. But the focus shifted to a single site: Skull Valley. The nuclear industry consortium and the federal government reasoned that although the Goshute reservation's 14,777 acres was a small plot, it was big enough to house all 44,000 tons of waste that had accumulated. All they needed to do was convince the twenty-five people from the five families that lived on the reservation (with another 155 members scattered around Utah and Nevada). How hard could that be? An hour west and south from Salt Lake City, the Goshute reservation is impoverished. PFS reasoned that many members of the tribe would embrace an infusion of cash, estimated at millions of dollars, in exchange for an affirmative vote. Besides, the storage "was only temporary."

Margene Bullcreek and fifteen other members of the Goshute people organized their own grassroots group to expose the new version of the deal that singled out Skull Valley and offered big cash rewards. She explained, "We wanted to create a precedent for other tribes to resist large amounts of money at the cost of destroying our heritage and the viability of our reservations." Their plan of sustained action began by creating an organized resistance—Ohngo Gaudadeh Devia (OGD)—on the reservation and letting the public know that many Native American people opposed the siting of the nuclear waste.

A major obstacle was the view of Leon Bear, who led the Tribal Council during the 1980s and '90s and favored accepting the placement of the spent fuel rods at Skull Valley. Millions of dollars were at stake. The realism of the official tribal leadership had a sad but understandable logic. Since the reservation was already surrounded by chemical polluters (Magnesium Corporation, the largest polluter in the United States, and Envirocare, a corporation that already received "low level" environmental waste, are nearby), tribal chairman Bear argued, in an article by Kevin Kamps for the Nuclear Information Service, "We can't do anything here that's green or environmental anyway. Would you buy a tomato from us if you knew what was already out here?" He argued that, in order to attract any type of development, the Goshute reservation would have to accept projects "consistent with what surrounds us." Some tribal members agreed: "Take the money, let's live in the present." Margene Bullcreek responded, "But what about the importance of small reservations, sovereignty, and self-determination? We need money but not that kind of money."

The OGD campaign pursued a strong philosophical, strategic, and spiritual message. Margene explained to me that they had to be steadfast and never relent in the face of false promises.

Sometimes we have to be reminded that who we are as Native Americans is the foundation of this struggle. There are teachings about why we were pushed into small reservations by the Europeans. I didn't go for the melting pot, assimilation plan that will destroy Native American culture, language, and our tra-

ditions of respecting the earth. I knew why there are
reservations. We are a spiritual people; the domineer-
ing society took all the best places with the best land
and abundant water. Our treaties gave us sovereignty.
But what of a dangerous accident? It would lead to
dispersion of our people and the end of the reservation which would become uninhabitable and the end
of our culture. It would lead to de-tribalization and
de-culturation.

In order to build for the strategy of sustained action, OGD
looked for support from allies in the Indigenous peoples
movement and from those in the dominant culture whose interests coincided in opposing the nuclear dumping.

The Indigenous Environmental Network helped to raise
funds and brought OGD to national environmental justice and
indigenous rights meetings, where they gained more allies
and received national television coverage. Winona LaDuke of
Honor the Earth, a Native-led organization, provided political
support and spoke out on their behalf. Margene felt strengthened by her eighteen-month participation in the American
Indian Lawyer Training Program, run by Larry Echohawk,
which helped her better understand both tribal and U.S. laws
so she could be an even more effective organizer. From 1992
to 2000, the Goshute were able to benefit from an environmental justice resolution—passed by the Clinton administration through the work of the national environmental justice
movement—that opposed the siting of hazardous waste and
other toxics in communities of color. However, during the
Bush administration that resolution was disregarded.

Again, the OGD realized their only hope was sustained
action. They challenged the decision of the Nuclear Regulatory Commission that the "dump is not violating environmental justice regulations" because of the large amount of money
being offered to the tribe. The OGD argued that no amount of
money could compensate for the damage to the integrity
of the tribe and its reservation.

Fortunately, there existed powerful tactical allies in Utah and Nevada, including governors and members of Congress. Nevada senator Harry Reid opposed any possible scenario that led to the Yucca Mountains becoming the ultimate "resting place," as the nuclear industry planned. The Yucca Mountains are Western Shoshone land and are supposed to be protected by their treaty rights. The government of Utah declared a local road leading to the Goshute reservation as a state road, thereby forcing the Private Fuel Storage consortium to get state approval to carry their products on trains and trucks. "The state put up a moat around the reservation to keep them out," Margene explained.

As the story of the danger became better publicized, many middle- and upper-class forces fought the siting as well. They did not want nuclear waste on the highways, train tracks, and roads that went through their communities. They became allies of the OGD sovereignty movement, if only out of a self-interest that they too saw the toxic future that nuclear transport and storage presented.

The OGD organizers learned to fight on another front—challenging corporate science. A common tactic among environmental polluters is to downplay the risk by giving specific projected "deaths per million" to measure cost-benefit for poisonous projects. This is done in the name of "risk assessment," a bizarre and pseudoscientific concept in which corporate scientists attempt to predict how many cancers per million, how many fatalities, or how many chances of a nuclear accident are the "costs" of siting a very dangerous toxic substance, such as nuclear fuel rods. The polluters actually would argue that ten, twenty, thirty deaths per million would justify a hazardous waste incinerator, a belching oil refinery, and a nuclear dump for spent fuel rods. But OGD and environmental justice groups all over the country countered this, often successfully. Fundamental to this counterargument is the environmental principle of "polluter pays;" that is, the polluters who cause the danger cannot also be the ones measuring its human costs and must assume the risk of their own production. It is also based on the internationally accepted "precautionary principle," which says that unless we are sure a chemical process does *not* cause cancer, related diseases, or a public health threat, we take the precaution not to introduce it into the environment in the first place.

OGD sponsored a high-visibility march, involving other tribes and supportive representatives of the governor's office, from the reservation to Salt Lake, a distance of seventy-seven miles. They showed that there were other forces on the reservation besides the tribal council leadership to speak for the Skull Valley Goshutes. They learned the art of media presentations and the power of an organized, dissenting voice on the reservation, which gave allies all over the country a cause to rally around.

In 2006, the Department of the Interior overruled a temporary agreement between the Goshute tribal leadership and PFS for siting of the nuclear waste. Two undersecretaries of the Department of the Interior ruled that the waste violated the culture and sovereignty of the tribe, and they prevented the siting on the grounds that Interior had the responsibility to protect the reservation and future generations of the Skull Valley. This was a direct response to the central argument that Margene Bullcreek and OGD had presented to them. Also, the PFS application was rejected because it did not address issues of accidents and other contingency planning to guarantee safety.

For several years after the 2006 ruling, the movement was not that active because it had, temporarily, won its objective. Yet nothing stands still in the realm of politics, and in January 2010, PFS went back to court to challenge the Department of the Interior ruling. On July 26, 2010, Judge David Ebel, in a federal district court in Salt Lake City, ruled that Interior had been "arbitrary and capricious" in blocking the agreement and sent it back for reconsideration. Supporters argue that the court ruling will eventually lead to the siting of the nuclear waste on Goshute land. Opponents interpret the decision that the Department of the Interior must give stronger documentation to its case, cross its t's and dot its i's, and then the Interior Department's ruling to prevent the siting will stand. Senator Orrin Hatch, a very conservative Republican, said, referring to the PFS application, "I thought we had put a stake through its heart forever," and indicated, along with the entire Utah congressional delegation, that he too would oppose its siting anywhere in the state.

The main conclusion is that, after twenty years of struggle, this story will not end for a long time, and the relentless forces opposing PFS and the nuclear storage plan will have to move into high gear again. As in all historical stories and great battles, there is no end—only temporary victories and defeats as long as both sides continue fighting. Margene Bullcreek and OGD say they are up for the task.

What would drive a dedicated group of tribal members on a tiny reservation to challenge their tribal council, Private Fuel Storage, the Department of Indian Affairs, the Department of the Interior, and the Department of Energy, and keep up the tactical offensive? Margene Bullcreek explained the core values that drive her style of work like this:

> The Europeans took our tribal leaders. No matter how hard they fought, many were eventually killed or driven into exile in Canada. They prayed for future generations and passed on to us that we have to continue to fight to preserve our culture and our people. Who am I to step outside myself, for it is how I was raised. We have ceremonies that are reinforced each day when the sun rises up every morning. When Columbus came, they took our land and imposed their church and their religion. They had wars and threw us in jail and massacred our people. The effort to put nuclear waste on Native land is only the latest chapter. We are still fighting for our land. That's what keeps me going.

In pursuit of profit, Private Fuel Storage keeps up the fight, day after day, decade after decade, willing to spend hundreds of millions of dollars in a desperate attempt to dump their nuclear waste. Out of political and spiritual necessity, Margene Bullcreek and the OGD from the Skull Valley Goshute people are relentless in defense of their land, sovereignty, and culture—for themselves and future generations.

Often, when public opinion is against them, the powerful forces approach the Goshute with the tactic "wear them down and wait them out." They assume, sometimes accurately, that grassroots groups, under-resourced and facing so many problems related to racism and poverty, cannot keep up the pressure year in and year out. In this case, the quality of relentlessness was reflected in a very long line of resistance—more than thirty years so far—a clear strategy, and an iron will, as seen in leaders like Margene Bullcreek and the larger Native American movement. The model of relentless resistance can encourage similar groups of underdogs all over the country.

Fights to Win:
Leading the Great Campaign

These are difficult times to navigate, and many organizations, doing dogged work, have often had to accept small victories, settlements, even straight out losses that have undermined their confidence. But organizers who fight to win hold fast to the belief that continually bigger and better change is possible, even under the darkest political clouds. Sometimes it's a combination of good fortune and good organizing, when the Red Sea opens up and for once the system grants major changes. These victories are not the private property of the organizations who win them. They are a gift to the movement. Some less-experienced but dedicated organizers can learn from these victories, learn from their mistakes, and readjust their tactical plan. Even some of the best-run campaigns have fought to win but have not won tactical reforms from the system. Sometimes the victory is simply the building of a stronger movement and consciousness. But in the midst of this challenging political terrain, it is wonderful when real victories in the conditions of working people can be won.

In our present historical period, waging the great campaign is the best vehicle for fighting to win. The great campaign is not a protest or an action but a long-term challenge to win power with very specific sets of fundamental, structural demands. It evolves over years and sometimes decades in a series of *campaigns within the campaign*. Organizers must be able to lead their organization on a long march, to learn the art of maneuver, of shifting the disposition of forces, of bringing new allies to the broad united front, of isolating the adversary and peeling possible allies away from them.

The organizers who led the struggle to end Jim Crow fought to win. It took thousands of campaigns waged over a century, but they did it. The U.S. movement to end the Vietnam War took twenty years. In their fight to win, the U.S. antiwar movement devised protests against Dow Chemical and ROTC, initiated draft-card burning and draft-resisters campaigns, organized soldiers in G.I. coffeehouses, built a Black soldiers movement inside the U.S. Army, ran peace candidates, and were able to nominate a Democratic candidate for president of the United States, George McGovern, the only truly antiwar candidate from a major party in U.S. history.

One of the most exciting great campaigns in recent years has been the battle of the Domestic Workers United in New York State to win a Domestic Workers Bill of Rights and build a national movement of domestic workers and excluded workers.

Ai-Jen Poo and the Domestic Workers United

In 1999, a few visionary organizers believed it was possible to bring dignity to domestic work and to New York City's 200,000 domestic workers. The idea of organizing the most exploited workers who were excluded from the labor laws was initiated by two organizations in New York: CAAAV—Organizing Asian Communities—and Andolan—Organizing South Asian Workers. These organizers began by reaching out to Caribbean and Latina women, including Beverly Alleyne, a nanny from Barbados who worked for a young family on New York's Upper

West Side, who said, "There is no place for us to go when our employers take advantage of us, so most of us stay silent." The women at these early meetings formed themselves into a steering committee, and Domestic Workers United (DWU) was born soon after, in 2000. Their lead organizer quickly became Ai-jen Poo, who had been organizing immigrant women workers since 1996 and was among the DWU's primary strategists and tacticians.

DWU's dream of a massive fighting group of organized Caribbean, Latino, and Asian domestic workers was a futuristic vision. The goal of winning major structural protections for domestic workers was initially dismissed by skeptics. Along with day laborers, farm workers, migrant laborers, and incarcerated workers, domestic workers belong to the class of "excluded workers," who have historically been excluded from the rights and protections of labor laws and traditional trade union organizing. But Ai-jen understood that, in order to fight to win, "we need that feeling that deep change, big change is really possible."

First, to support the belief that deep change is possible, the organizers began with an analysis of the condition of domestic workers in the United States. They considered the history of patriarchy, the way it has made all domestic labor invisible. They also connected labor exclusion to the exploitation of Black slave labor. Labor organizing in the 1930s was shaped by these sexist and racist roots. At the height of Franklin Roosevelt's New Deal, in 1935, Congress passed the National Labor Relations Act, which gave workers the right to organize unions. Domestic workers and farmworkers were explicitly excluded from the protections of the act. In the early part of the twentieth century, most of the nation's domestic workers and farmworkers were Black. Southern Democrats in Congress blocked their labor rights out of fear that an alliance of Black and white workers might organize, not just to challenge their employers but also the system of Jim Crow segregation itself. As Ai-jen Poo put it, "The combination of these dynamics—the racialized exclusion of domestic workers from labor laws, the gendered devaluation of women's work in the home, the decentralized structure of the industry, and the economic pressures facing immigrants from the global South—makes domestic workers extremely vulnerable to exploitation and abuse."

Moving from analysis to action in the earliest stage of the great campaign can be most difficult. In order to build consciousness and group cohesiveness, DWU and their many legal partners, such as the Urban Justice Center, sued abusive employers, winning claims from back pay totaling $450,000. Out of this momentum, DWU and allies organized to get the New York City Council to pass a labor law compelling employment agencies to educate domestic workers and employers about basic industry rights. At the high point of this campaign, DWU and their sister organizations filled every seat in the balcony of the city council chambers during the legislative hearings.

While many would savor such a victory and be satisfied, in 2003, DWU worked to build on the New York victory and escalate the demands. They spent thousands of hours organizing hundreds of domestic workers from across the state—an impressive feat in itself—to gather for a meeting given in six languages. It was at this meeting that participants initiated the idea for a statewide Domestic Workers Bill of Rights. This bill would have much more muscle than the earlier labor law: a minimum of one day of rest per week, a $14-an-hour living wage, health care, notice of termination, severance pay, paid holidays, paid leave, and protection from discrimination.

In a few short years, DWU built an impressive grassroots base, the vast majority of whom were immigrant women from Central America and the Caribbean; generated a citywide profile; won benefits for workers; passed a New York City ordinance; and set their goals higher on a major labor victory—no matter how many years it would take to win.

The art of this campaign hinged on a synthesis of influencing members of the New York state legislature who would ultimately have to pass the bill, building the base of the domestic workers themselves and preparing them for a long-term campaign, and dramatically expanding the allies of Domestic Workers United to create a statewide movement that could generate enough votes to win. By now the leadership team had been expanded. Organizers like Christine Lewis, Angelica Fernandez, Deloris Wright, Joycelyn Gill-Campbell, Lois Newland, Patricia Francois, Marilyn Blackett, Allison Julien, Barbara Young, and dozens more—all domestic workers and women of color—made up a solid leadership base to lead this long-term campaign.

There are many factors that led to the victory by the steering committee—a group of organizers fighting to win—that warrant attention. First, they won the battle of ideas. Opponents of the bill argued that domestic workers should bargain collectively like other workers. DWU answered that domestic workers were specifically excluded from collective bargaining laws. Also, they typically worked alone, with a one-person employer, and thus would face retaliation or firing if they complained or tried to negotiate with an abusive employer. The only form of "collective bargaining" had to be in the form of statewide legal protections for all 200,000 domestic workers.

Second, DWU put domestic workers in front of the march. Legislators were moved by those directly impacted leading the struggle. DWU organized legislative days in Albany, the state capital, led by domestic workers captains like Allison Julien, who came from Barbados and followed two generations of domestic workers in her mother and grandmother. Legislators, in general, respond well to organized forces, and the DWU leaders were able to document employer abuses that were systematic—withholding pay, refusing sick days or personal days, or preventing domestic workers from leaving the house to go home to care for their own children. Pat Francois documented in photos evidence of a beating she received at the hands of an employer when she intervened to stop him from hitting his own child.

DWU then made a conscious decision that it needed to

broaden the grand coalition to win the victory. One component of its tactical plan was to set out to win the hearts of many of the very employers they were seeking to regulate. Millions of New Yorkers had relatives who were domestic workers or were raised by nannies or had housekeeping help. By building an alliance of the oppressed and the more privileged members of society, they avoided an us-versus-them struggle, as in, "all employers are exploitative, all workers are exploited." While in most cases that was true, DWU chose to build up the support of the progressive employers, and that discouraged the worst employers to organize against them.

By framing the issue in terms of "exclusion" from basic labor rights and recognition, DWU made allies with women's organizations, which had long protested the unpaid and underpaid work of women in the home. They allied with farmworker organizations, which also were excluded from union protection; with unemployed and homeless groups; and with faith leaders, who saw DWU's great campaign as part of a larger human rights movement. DWU built an alliance of children who were raised by nannies, children of domestic workers, and adults whose childhood had been shaped positively by domestic workers. Picket signs read, "Respect My Mom" and "My nanny takes me to the zoo." Children asked the governor to sign the bill because, "My mom works hard, she deserves respect," and children asked to be able to spend more time with their own mothers.

In 2007, Ai-jen Poo and Barbara Young, a domestic worker and former union leader in her native Barbados, reached out to then–AFL-CIO president John Sweeney to see if he could bring the power of the ten-million-member union to the domestic workers' cause. Sweeney's mother had been a domestic worker for forty years and experienced the pain of being unable to organize or have federal or state protections. Sweeney pledged to join the workers at a rally and lobbying day in Albany, and, unlike many union and elected officials, he actually kept his promise. The Democratic members of the state senate, who constituted a majority, were impressed that

Sweeney chose to get involved in a statewide issue, and DWU gained even more credibility.

Ai-jen Poo explains the core of DWU's organizing theory: "Every one of us has needed care, provided care, or relied on someone else for care at some point in our lives. If we frame our work around values and create the right conditions, people will choose fairness and love even when it cuts against their immediate self-interest."

A key alliance was built between the Domestic Workers and the Shalom Bayit project of Jews for Racial and Economic Justice. The groups reached out to Jewish employers of domestic help and from there to a number of synagogues to make the workers' rights a high priority for progressive Jews. In moving style, Gayle Kirschenbaum, an employer, explained to legislators that when her son's caretaker referred to her as boss, she did not like it, wishing it wasn't so. But it was exactly what the relationship was. "My resistance to seeing myself as an employer meant that it took too long for Debbie to be treated as an employee," Kirschenbaum said. "Rather than signing a contract and agreeing on the terms on day one, we talked about benefits casually, after she'd already started work. I would not have tolerated such lack of professionalism in my own job."

The work of influential rabbis attracted to the cause led to a meeting between DWU and the speaker of the New York State Assembly, Sheldon Silver. Now the years of organizing began to take a sharper legislative focus. This in turn led to more media coverage and opportunities for DWU organizers to tell their stories to an increasingly aware and sympathetic public. When they were on the Brian Lehrer radio program, Lehrer called New York governor David Paterson to put him on the spot about the Domestic Workers Bill of Rights. To everyone's surprise, the governor said, "The exclusion of domestic workers and farmworkers from labor rights is the legacy of a long history of racism. When this bill comes to my desk, I will sign it." And he did.

On July 1, 2010, ten years after the formation of Domestic

Workers United, and seven years after they initiated the campaign, the Domestic Workers Bill of Rights—which provides overtime pay, protection from discrimination, and other employment benefits for more than 200,000 domestic workers—became law.

Ai-jen Poo led DWU in defining a long-term strategy—to build a large movement of previously unorganized domestic workers to challenge the employers and win a statewide labor rights bill. They went on a journey to build the great campaign, which Ai-jen Poo likens to "a great love affair," which in fact was based on tough-minded politics that constantly adjusted the tactical plan to unite all who could be united and to isolate and even neutralize the adversaries. As Ai-jen explains in the DWU publication "Organizing with Love: Lessons from the New York Domestic Workers Bill of Rights Campaign," the DWU kept winning the battle of ideas, expanded its constituency and statewide allies, and created a new organized force in New York.

At every high and low point of their ten-year struggle, the DWU refused to be satisfied with partial victories or to sit down when defeated. There are 2.5 million domestic workers in the United States—we can only imagine the shock waves DWU will set off in other cities and states.

And the organizers continue to fight to win: they organized a new National Domestic Workers Alliance at a congress at the United States Social Forum in Atlanta in 2007, which has grown to thirty-three member organizations in seventeen cities. Further, at the second U.S. Social Forum, in Detroit in June 2010, the National Domestic Workers Alliance coalesced with farmworkers, restaurant workers, guest workers, day laborers, taxi drivers, workfare workers, and the formerly incarcerated in the first-ever Excluded Workers Congress to share organizing strategies and address the new challenges to collective bargaining for the working-class majority of the twenty-first century.

The DWU is one of the great success stories of the second decade of the twenty-first century because it mastered the long march and the art of the great campaign. As it expands its vision nationally, DWU continues to fight to win. Organizers throughout the United States should study this history well, for it is in the microcosm of great victories that we can deduce a lot of lessons to help us fight to win too.

CONCLUSION

*The Time for Transformative
Organizing Is Now!*

On May 17, 2010, five students entered the Tucson office of Arizona senator John McCain and began a sit-in, risking deportation to fight for federal legislation known as the Dream Act that would give undocumented high school students the opportunity to attend college and be eligible for citizenship. Declaring, "We are undocumented and unafraid," immigrants Lizbeth Mateo of Los Angeles; Tania Unzueta of Chicago; Mohammad Abdollahi of Ann Arbor, Michigan; and Yahaira Carillo of Kansas City, along with Arizona native Raul Alcaraz, occupied the office for seven hours before they were arrested. Three of them were held in Immigration and Customs Enforcement (ICE) detention centers, the worst in the country.

Lizbeth explained why the Dream Act is so important. Born in Mexico, she came to the United States when she was fourteen. She had to learn English and adapt to a whole new culture. California law allows undocumented students who attend high school in the state to go to college at in-state tuition rates. Lizbeth was admitted to California State University at Northridge, where she graduated with a major in

Chicana/o studies. But then she hit a wall: "So here is the problem," she says. "I have a degree, but it's virtually impossible for me to get a job." The Dream Act would give students like Lizbeth six years of conditional legal status while they go to school or serve in the military, and then put them on a path to permanent citizenship.

The Dream Act 5, as they were known, were booked and released the day after their arrest, but they are still under ICE authority and have to report to the agency every month as they wait for it to decide what action to bring against them. Their militant sit-in has sparked similar actions by immigrant youth all over the country, including a thousand undocumented young people who staged a mock graduation at the White House in July 2010. Theirs are the most militant and widespread reflections of Chicano youth protest today. In Los Angeles alone in 2010, eleven demonstrators are facing charges for nonviolent civil disobedience in support of the Dream Act. Twenty-five additional demonstrators are facing charges for a major demonstration that tied up traffic for hours protesting Arizona's Senate Bill 1070, which has led to mass arrests of undocumented workers. It was time to take action and, for some, to put their bodies on the line.

"I have worked for the Dream Act from the time I was nineteen till today, when I am twenty-six," says Lizbeth. "Many have lost hope. Many live in fear. This country prides itself on equal rights and being 'a nation of immigrants,' but our people are being hunted down."

I asked Lizbeth if she had any regrets.

"I did what I did consciously," she says. "There is no room for regrets; the risks were worth it. The community support has been overwhelming and my parents pray for me. We had to be a catalyst to show Congress the courage they didn't have. We need more of you to march, to write letters, to risk arrest and, if necessary, jail time. Will you join us?!"

I started this book with the story of a young Black man from the Student Nonviolent Coordinating Committee putting his body on the line for the civil rights revolution. I end with a young Latina from the immigrant rights movement putting her body on the line, forty-six years later. The fundamental question remains: *"Are you ready to join the social justice revolution?"*

Now that you have read this far, let's look at the world in which we are organizing, the coordinates of hope, and the tasks in front of us. Let's look at what we can do to strengthen a movement for transformative organizing.

What is the challenge?

Successful organizing begins with a sober analysis of the conditions within which we are working.

We all know that the system that engulfs our lives and our work is in another massive crisis, and a permanent decline. The United States depends on its war economy, as it has to accept a diminished role in a multipolar world, in which Russia, China, Brazil, and India are claiming huge markets. Now we face global economic, environmental, and political crises.

Sixteen million people are now unemployed, and at least 50 million people live below the poverty line—part of the low-wage, no-wage working class. Mass unemployment is becoming permanent. As the stock market rebounds through government subsidy, a "workerless recovery" shrinks the private sector. Housing, food, and water are increasingly costly, and foreclosures, evictions, poverty, and hunger are on the rise. The social welfare state we fought for and have relied upon even as services declined is shredded—aid to families, mental health clinics, county hospitals, trauma centers have disappeared; people are cold, sick, and hungry and left on their own to survive. We are increasingly suffering the undeniable manifestations of the ecological crisis. The recent scorching heat in Russia and the floods in Pakistan have continued the trajectory of Hurricane Katrina's destructive force. There is a collision course between the greed and rationalizations of the West and the force of nature; science and the planet are the casualties. The United States is involved in wars in Iraq and Afghanistan, and has a network of 800 military bases.

Where is the hope?

The tradition of transformative organizing always finds the paths of hope. In dark times, what do we do? We organize.

Radical organizing grows in times of despair. The union movement grew during the Great Depression, the Civil Rights Movement grew during the height of segregation, the anti–Vietnam War movement grew at a time when the United States was bombing civilian populations, and the African National Congress grew at the height of apartheid. In our recent history, we saw massive antiwar marches in the millions all over the world against the U.S. invasion of Iraq in 2003. In 2006, millions of people marched for immigrant rights. In 2007, thirty thousand people marched in Louisiana in support of the Jena 6—six high school youth accused of beating up a white student in the midst of intense racial harassment. Through mass public support from all over the country, it became one of the largest civil rights marches about a single incident since the 1960s.

And then in 2008, hundreds of thousands of activists came forward and were transformed into organizers who in turn moved some 2 million people to campaign for and elect a Black president they believed would stand up to and reverse the legacy of Bush and Cheney. The campaign to elect Barack Obama was a watershed in U.S. history and reflected a revolution of on-the-ground organizing. Obama's army of 2 million—which exploded into systematic phone banking and people holding house meetings with their neighbors and going door-to-door in swing states to talk to voters they had never met—ended up changing many minds. The Obama electoral movement was one of the great political alliances in U.S. history and led to the election of the first Black president of the United States—who ran on a progressive platform.

Many of us joined the campaign to fight for civil rights and against the war in Iraq; for universal, single-payer health care; and for the expansion of social programs. In a heartening turn of events, 96 percent of Black voters, 80 percent of Native American voters, 67 percent of Latino voters, 62 percent of Asian American voters, and 46 percent of white voters supported Obama for president. Even more encouraging as a trend is that 56 percent of white voters aged eighteen to twenty-nine voted for a Black man with an African name against a white man who wrapped himself in the flag.

Significant numbers of the best and brightest who worked for Obama are seeking out transformative organizations that are building an independent political base to pressure the president from the left and face the Tea Party on the right. The victory of the Obama electoral campaign is a permanent victory for the social movement Left and proves that it is possible to build a progressive mass movement in the United States today. It is from this undeniable historical phenomenon that future hope can be built.

In this context, it is the urgent and unique role of a democratic Left to build a movement independent of and to the left of the Democratic Party; to push both parties from that grassroots base, to find opportunity to unite with the Obama administration when possible, and to challenge the administration when necessary; to protect the president from racist attack, to unite with Democratic progressives, to ally with the center and moderates in a united front against the Right, and to focus on "demand development" for an independent political program that places the interests of working people and communities of color at the center.

Progressives also draw great hope from social movements that have multiplied around the world, with campaigns for arable land, clean and free water, clean air, food security, and self-determination from U.S. transnational corporations and the U.S. military. While global capitalism declines, many countries are rejecting the neoliberal economy that has forced them over the decades into debt and chaos. A vibrant twenty-first-century movement for self-determination and ecological sustainability is rising in Venezuela, Ecuador, and Bolivia, encouraged by Brazil, which is developing new forms of economic and political cooperation to demonstrate an alternative to the U.S. model of exploitation.

The international focus of U.S. organizing has been on the rise. Forums around the globe and within the United States are gathering large numbers of organizers, rooted in real struggles, building international ties, coalescing to build their strength. In Detroit in June 2010, eighteen thousand organizers attended the U.S. Social Forum, where workshops on transformative organizing had standing-room-only attendance. There were also many international forums at the USSF initiated by Grassroots Global Justice Alliance and various Third World groups. And groups asking for the removal of U.S. bases from their territories, such as Colombia and Guahan (Guam), were pleased to find many of USSF participants supportive of their demands. As international alliances have grown, movement organizers have invited more international guests to the United States to become familiar with our movements in support of self-determination for nations all around the world. Progressive organizers gather at United Nations events, NGO (nongovernmental organizations) gatherings, World Social Forum *encuentros,* hemispheric alliances, and actions led by groups such as the World March of Women. These nascent international alliances provide the seeds of a winning strategy.

The theory of transformative organizing is based on the premise that the kinds of progressive demands discussed throughout this book are in the interests of working people and of much of the middle class in the United States, and in the ethical interests of all of us. Practice shows us that when organizers take these demands into their workplaces, communities, schools, and houses of worship, we can successfully organize around them. This approach is based on the belief in the intelligence and capacity of working people, people of color, and students to listen to new ideas contrary to the dominant U.S. master narrative. Organizers need to study, practice, and learn to make the case to end the U.S. blockade of Cuba, or for the United States to close down its military bases, or for the U.S. government to demand the most drastic reductions in greenhouse gases.

Of course it takes good agitation, good political education, performance art, e-organizing, masterful leaflets, and great and persuasive one-on-one conversations to accomplish this too. When the war in Vietnam first came to popular attention, the vast majority of people in the United States were initially for it. But as antiwar organizers, we found that support for the war was a mile wide and an inch deep—when presented with facts, political, and moral arguments, masses of people joined the antiwar movement.

The demands raised by the organizers profiled in this book give a framework for a comprehensive politics. There is a gaping political hole in the U.S. body politic to the left of the Tea Party that the official leadership of the Democratic Party does not want to take up. A powerful social movement, including many Democratic voters, must be willing and able to fill that vacuum. These demands provide a counter-hegemonic challenge to the system, a coherent program that we can take out on the block, out on the bus, worker to worker, and door to door.

How will you answer the call?

The exciting thing about being an organizer is there is little room or time for despair. There is always room for optimism; there is always something to do that is historically important, choices in one's life that matter, a challenge against more powerful foes, great people to work with, and a real chance for victory. Here are some concrete steps every reader can take.

Join an organization and become involved. Move from being a person who attends a march to someone who joins an organization and is in the office working on the logistics and making the march happen, from handing out leaflets to helping write them, from making donations to raising funds from your networks, and from attending a monthly meeting to protecting at least eight hours a week to make your social commitment qualitatively more effective. Build your progressive organization. Social movements cannot grow or merge with others unless we as organizers understand the critical importance of building the peoples' institutions.

Make a move to be more strategically positioned in society. Some people cannot change cities or jobs to join the organization they think best. Some can. If you want to be the most effective organizer, think about where you want to work and live. *Wherever you are, make strategic life choices to keep you close to society's most oppressed and energetic.* Are you working in the same factory where your mom or dad worked? Join the union or help organize one. Are you seeking a socially responsible job? Become a public school teacher, nurse's aide, nurse, or doctor in a low-income clinic, county hospital, or AIDS center, where you can make contacts with workers and patients to fight for better medical services. If you are a teacher, administrator, maintenance worker, student, or parent, you are strategically situated to fight against privatized education and for antiracist, progressive public school education. If your organization is focusing on a particular constituency or there is a neighborhood that you want to impact, consider changing your job or moving to be closer to the base you organize. Only a few people can make a living as a full-time organizer, but millions of people can devote their lives to organizing within the contours of work, family, health, and politicizing the daily experiences of their lives.

Understand your life from an organizer's perspective. Are your friends or family trapped by the criminal justice system? Given that there are more than 2 million people in U.S. prisons, 1 million of whom are Black and 500,000 Latino, and estimating that each prisoner has five or more family members directly impacted, that means there are 10 million

Build a deep base. Is your organization building a strong grassroots base? The new regional, national, and international movements we need cannot happen unless the organizers coming together have a strong base in communities, churches, synagogues, mosques, workplaces, public schools, and universities. I remember during the height of the anti–Vietnam War movement in the late 1960s, I was one of 500,000 marchers on the Fifth Avenue Peace Parade in New York. Each delegation—Bedford-Stuyvesant, Jamaica, Upper West Side, Harlem, South Bronx, Staten Island—marched proudly against the war. Teamsters, auto workers, doctors, psychiatrists, nurses—against the war. High schools, hospitals, elderly centers—against the war. A movement of this scale cannot happen without organizers going door–to-door, person-to-person, in lunch rooms, at break times to build constituencies. Going deep into one community and generating some level of saturation is critical. For once you are in the high schools, the key neighborhoods, known in the churches and synagogues, in cultural centers and workplaces, and on the media, you begin to make a qualitative leap in the impact of your influence, which sporadic efforts will never achieve.

Seek out national networks of organizations doing great work. If you are in a vital grassroots organization, it's essential to build alliances to strengthen the campaigns you are organizing, Alliances also enable organizations to work beyond their own projects: groups working on civil rights can align with others focusing on women's rights; groups working against gentrification can join campaigns designed by others that fight immigrant detention centers; organizations fighting for a civil rights amendment to federal transportation legislation can also join in international delegations to the United Nations. The Grassroots Global Justice Alliance is a network of fifty-three groups doing important work in low-income communities of color and playing a major role in international conferences and movement building. The National Domestic Workers Alliance is reaching out to workers in every state and can use your help. So can other key national networks such as the National Day Laborer Organizing Network, Indigenous Environmental Network, Right to the City, Transit Riders for Public Transportation, Transportation Equity Network, National Lawyers Guild, Push Back Network, Jobs with Justice, Coalition of Immokalee Workers, Malcolm X Grassroots Movement, Take Back the Land, Iraq Veterans Against the War (which includes veterans of the war in Afghanistan), and Women Organizing Women. Democrats.com and BoldProgressives.org are doing important e-organizing, raising funds and turning out phone bankers for insurgent Democrats against conservative Democrats in the primaries, and then backing progressive Democrats in the general election against reactionary Republicans. These are just a sample of the excellent groups working at the national level

The exciting breakthrough today is the growing collaboration among regional, national, and international networks where groups must come in with a strong base, can retain some of their autonomy, but sign up for a higher level of cooperation in which agreements are made and implemented. Once you sign up, your energetic participation is expected and our power grows.

Spread an international net. Those of us who are organizing inside the United States need to get outside in order to even begin to grasp what this country looks like to activists in other countries. Many organizations understand this and send delegations to international meetings to lend solidarity to important struggles of resistance to the policies of our government and of U.S. corporations.

While the United Nations is a complex arena under tremendous control of the United States, the Security Council and General Assembly are still important arenas where the stakes are high and some important resolutions have actually changed conditions on the ground in terms of government accountability on trade, toxics, greenhouse gases, and Indigenous rights. The NGOs work tirelessly to eke out progressive language from governments who often have no intention of following it. Perhaps the most instructive experience is to see the way governments all over the world are exclaiming, "What are we going to do about the United States?!" and how much hope they place on U.S. grassroots movements to stand up to the destructive policies of our own government.

The World Social Forums are important arenas for social movement gatherings. The WSF is not a decision-making body and, in some ways, has restricted the scope of its conversations by the exclusion of political parties and governments. Still, WSF provides organizers with excellent opportunities to hear advanced ideas and to network with other groups to reach real operative agreements—often resulting in delegations visiting each other's countries and in commitments to read each other's publications and learn from each other's practice.

Participation in international gatherings that address specific issues is increasingly possible. In April 2010, Bolivian president Evo Morales initiated the World People's Conference on Climate Change and the Rights of Mother Earth in Cochabamba to develop a powerful grassroots counter program to bring to the UN Framework Convention on Climate Change. Focusing on enforceable regulations to reduce greenhouse gas emissions to 50 percent of 1990 levels, this proposal is light years ahead of the United States' and European Union's emphasis on voluntary, unverifiable levels.

As you look for a group to join or a direction for the group you are in, ask yourself: "What is our international strategy and what work are we doing to link the struggles of people in the United States to people all over the world?"

Create movement convergences and build movement centers. The U.S. Social Forums held in Atlanta in 2007 and in Detroit in 2010 exemplified the movement-building atmosphere we need to create on a daily basis. And the scale of an 18,000-person gathering of 1,700 organizations gives us a glimpse of what a *movement of social movements* can look like. In your city, at national events, or during international convenings, introduce a cultural engine for our movement— places to gather: convergence spaces like La Peña Cultural Center in Berkeley, California, training camps, and children's playgrounds; art-making centers like Self-Help Graphics in Los Angeles; venues like the Leftist Lounge in Detroit and the Brecht Forum in New York; and movement movie theaters, where activists and organizers can attend, encouraging political films and building their audience. We need a collective movement life that is a visible and accessible presence in the cities and rural areas where we organize. We need venues where different races, classes, gender expressions, and languages can come together to discuss strategy and tactics—where cultural performers can build their audience. We need online organizers who are skilled at crossing cultural boundaries so that there is a common set of spaces that the movement occupies and that are attended by all.

It's time to make history together

The challenge posed throughout this book is to develop the qualities that will make us all successful organizers. *Playbook for Progressives* is a call for *Movement Building*—*building a Movement of social movements*. My hope is that you will integrate these qualities into a strategy for transformative organizing. Transformative organizing works to structurally transform the system, transform the consciousness of the people being organized, and, in the process, transform the consciousness of the organizer. It is the backbone and the model of what we are fighting for and how we can succeed in that battle

The Movement we are seeking is only now coming into being. Though we all share a vision of a world beyond oppression, there are differences and contradictions between different peoples and between social movements—some because of political disagreements; some because of cultural, gender, class, and racial conflicts; and in other cases because the system has set us against each other. Given the class and race stratification and segregation of our society, people doing social justice work often identify with their particular cause and do not know each other or see themselves as part of a common movement. This is to the grave detriment of our organizing work.

In the present period of intensifying government repression, we need to develop relationships where people know each other by name and approach our work in coalitions, networks, alliances, and a united front as a life-and-death issue. If the police round up the most dedicated activists and organizers, it will be essential to have built broad and deep alliances with many forces in the city, region, and nation that can fight to free them from the custody of the police and the courts through mass action and first-rate legal defense. People fight for people they know, and we have to make a systematic effort to support each other's causes, attend each other's events, and fight for each other's interests, as well as those we share in common.

Given the difficult conditions facing us and the vision we all share, I propose that the task for progressive organizers is to coalesce our disparate arenas of work into a broad Movement for Global Justice: an international united front against racism, the police state, ecological destruction, and war led by a strategic alliance of forces building bases on the ground, centered in working-class communities of color, and expanding to all classes and races in society.

We need to continue holding movement convergences and conferences on what to do about global warming, the mass incarceration of Black and Brown people, the growing attacks on women's rights to control their own bodies, attacks on the very existence of LGBTQ peoples, the breaking of unions, the constant wars of occupation and terrorism against civilians, and the repression against movement building in the United States perpetrated under the "Homeland Security" banner.

Yes, these are difficult days. That is why the time for Transformative Organizing is now. More than ever, you and I and we are needed to organize for a global justice agenda and build a new Movement. We are all needed to answer the call.

ACKNOWLEDGMENTS

My life has been a process of collective work. I am very appreciative of Gayatri Patnaik, Joanna Green, and the Beacon Press board for believing in this project and giving it the light of day. My editor, Joanna Green, has provided structure and insight into my work. She has always been on my side and was instrumental in getting this project to the finish line. My managing editor, Susan Lumenello, brought greater sentence-by-sentence clarity that strengthened the line of argument.

Daniel Won-gu Kim graduated from the National School for Strategic Organizing in 2001, and he commuted from Denver to Los Angeles to push the completion of Playbook from 2007 to 2010. As a scholar and writer, he willed me on to write when I needed encouragement and focus.

Lian Hurst Mann is my partner in everything and is my advisor, mentor, and comrade. After thirty-five years together, it's hard to figure out where her ideas start and my ideas end—we are so much a product of collective practice. She played a critical role in refining the politics of the book.

Daniel, Lian, and I found a groove working together and went over every piece before we sent it to Joanna, who then took it to another level of clarity and sharpness—we all functioned as successful organizers in the production of this book.

•   •   •

My grandmother, Sarah Mandell, was a Russian Jewish immigrant who fled the pogroms in 1910. She came to the United States, where she worked in a sweatshop and helped form the International Ladies Garment Workers Union. My father, Howard Mann, was a union organizer and socialist. My mother, Libby Mann, was a feminist and socialist and my ethical mentor. I am very appreciative to them for bringing me into the world and exposing me to the ideas that would shape my life.

This is the book I have been writing for many years, although other books have taken precedence. Apparently this is finally the time to complete it. I have been committed to left movement-building all my life and have spent more than four decades as a civil rights, antiwar, labor, and environmental organizer. I have had so many teachers and mentors, and have been a student all my life. My greatest friends have been my best comrades in The Movement, and I am indebted to all of them for shaping *Playbook for Progressives: 16 Qualities of the Successful Organizer* through their own organizing practice. Some of them are characters in my book; many others influenced my thinking and are thanked here to recognize their formative contributions.

In the **Congress of Racial Equality,** I am indebted to Lou Smith who hired me, the late Herb Callender, Ed Day, Dave Dennis, the late James Farmer, Joyce Ware, , the late George Wiley, and the late James Chaney, Andrew Goodman, and Mickey Schwerner. I am also deeply appreciative of the work of Jim Peck and other CORE Freedom Riders and to the Trailways workers Eddie Barnes, Noel Quiñones, and Big Sam.

In the **Newark Community Union Project,** Jesse Allen, Daisy Ash, Steve Block, Connie Brown, Corinna Fales, George Fontaine, Carol Glassman, Tom Hayden, Melvin Higgins, David Hungerford, Phil Hutchings, Nancy Ingraham, Terry Jefferson, Marian Kidd, Wyla McClain, Betty Moss, Louise

Patterson, George Richardson, Bessie Smith, Thurman Smith, and Anita Warren supported and elevated my work.

In **Students for a Democratic Society,** I am very grateful to Fran Ansley, Karen Ashley, Ellen Bravo, Sarah Driscoll, Roxanne Dunbar, Susan Hagedorn, the late Abbie Hoffman, Craig Kaplan, the late Murray Levin, Sandy Lillydahl, Marge Piercy, the late Howard Zinn, my brother, Richard Mann, who was of great support, and my daughter, Lisa, who at three traveled around New England with me on buses as I worked as a "regional traveler" to help build SDS chapters.

United Auto Workers: I worked on UAW assembly lines for a decade at the Ford Milpitas, GM Southgate, and GM Van Nuys plants and was helped by New Directions leaders Jerry Tucker and the late Victor and Sophie Reuther and by UAW Local 645 leaders Pete Beltran, Jake Flukers, Mike Gomez, Manuel Hurtado, Kelly Jenco, and Mark Masaoka, who provided companionship and never let me walk alone.

Labor/Community Coalition to Keep GM Van Nuys Open: in the predecessor to the Strategy Center, I was trained by Rudy Acuña, Ed Asner, Jorge Garcia, the late Rev. Frank Higgins, Nadine Kerner, Jack Koszdin, the late Father Luis Olivares, and the late Eloy Salazar.

I have been with the **Labor/Community Strategy Center** for more than twenty years. So many people helped us build the scaffolding, the foundation, and floor after floor of a still-growing structure: Lisa Adler, Maria Aguirre, Kelly Archbold, Elena Astilleros, Damon Azali-Rojas, Kirti Baranwal, Tanya Bernard, Della Bonner, Sanyika Bryant, Rita Burgos, Tom Camarella, Gilbert Cedillo, Woodrow Coleman, Manuel Criollo, Patrisse Cullors, the late Pearl Daniels, Dan DiPasquo, Lisa Durán, Amos Dyson, the late Pat Elmore, the late Mytyl Gomboske, Carla Gonzalez, Maria Guardado, Stephen Gutwillig, Cynthia Hamilton, Georgia Hayashi, the late Ted Hays, Norma Henry, Martín Hernández, Carol Jackson, Mark-Anthony Johnson, the late Cirilo Juarez, Daniel Kim, Grandma Hee Pok Kim, Kate Kinkade, Bianca Kovar, Richard Larson, Nancy Lawrence, Lissett Lazo, Bill Lann Lee, Alejandra Lemus, Joe Linton,

Barbara Lott-Holland, Tammy Bang Luu, Lian Hurst Mann, Esperanza Martinez, Chris Mathis, Rosalio Mendiola, the late Dick Meyers, Scott Miller, Sonissa Norman, Peter Olney, Deborah Orosz, Alex Caputo Pearl, Shepherd Petit, Rudy and Rosa Pisani, Francisca Porchas, Michele Prichard, Laura Pulido, Geoff Ramsey-Ray, Kikanza Ramsey-Ray, Patrick Ramsey, Judi Redman, Connie Rice, Ted Robertson, Cynthia Rojas, Eric Romann, Gloria Romero, Tom Rubin, Palak Shah, Ryan Snyder, Dae-Han Song, Erica Teasley, Andy Terranova, Anthony Thigpenn, Dean Toji, Layla Welborn, Kendra Williby, Sunyoung Yang, and Ricardo and Noemi Zelada. I want to thank Francisca, Manuel, and Tammy for taking up additional leadership roles and responsibilities to allow me to finish this book.

Then there are old friends and others made along the way who are part of my support circle as advisors, confidantes, and comrades: Aris and Isaura Anagnos, Sam Anderson, Patricia Bauman, Rachel Beller, Jaron Browne, Bob Bullard, Charlotte Bullock, Robin Cannon, the late Luke Cole, Cecil Corbin-Mark, Gary Delgado, Michelle DePass, Tom and Janis Dutton, Juliet Ellis, Reese Erlich, Leslie Fields, Rich Finigan, Bill Fletcher, Bill Gallegos, Fernando Gapasin, Juana and Ricardo Gutierrez, Inez Hedges, Anne Hess, Fred Ho, the late David Hunter, Glenn Johnson, Robin D. G. Kelley, Jay Levin, the late Manning Marable, Mildred McClain, Mauricio Michaels, Vernice Miller, Carlos Montes, Richard Moore, Ai-jen Poo, Doris Puehringer, Rinku Sen, Peggy Shephard, Peter and Phyllis Skaller, the late Damu Smith, Hoby Spalding, Angel Torres, Swamy Venuturupalli, Victor Wallis, Haskell Wexler, Beverly Wright, and Haeyoung Yoon.

Lian and I have been able to integrate a loving family and passionate politics. Lian's mother, Melinda Hurst, has been a dear friend and advocate from the first day I met her. Our daughters, Celia and Melinda, are working in the inner city and have been constant supporters of our work. Our sons-in-law, Joe Ward-Wallace and Maurice Rivera, are regulars at the

Strategy Center political parties and have expanded the project of our family's work. My brother- and sister-in-law, Hank and Mindy Askin, have been rooting me on. It really does take a village to get just one book done. And our grandkids, Ava, Ethan, Josh, Layla, and Raider, are part of the billions of youth all over the world who deserve and demand a better and healthier future.

While I have learned from many people throughout my life, no mention of an organization or individual constitutes their endorsement of my views as presented in this book. The synthesis remains my own and my responsibility.

This book was written, as Marge Piercy has said, "to be of use" to organizers all over the world. I look forward with excitement to hearing feedback from my comrades in Harlem and Johannesburg, Phoenix and Berlin, Compton and Caracas, Kensington and Kuala Lumpur, and my many comrades from the grassroots movements operating at the United Nations and the World Social Forum. We urgently need a mass movement for peace and social justice. I welcome the discussion, debate, deliberation, and demonstrations; the caucusing, campaigns, and coalitions; and the broad united front against racism, ecological destruction, war, and empire that I hope this book encourages and moves forward.